The Pigeon Shooter

A Complete Guide to Modern Pigeon Shooting

JOHN BATLEY

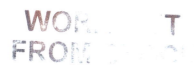

SWAN·HILL
PRESS

First published in the UK in 1996
by Swan Hill Press, an imprint of Airlife Publishing Ltd

This edition published 1999

British Library Cataloguing in Publication Data
  A catalogue record for this book
  is available from the British Library

ISBN 1 84037 125 0

Typeset by Hewer Text Composition Services, Edinburgh
Printed in England by Butler & Tanner Ltd, Frome and London

Swan Hill Press
an imprint of Airlife Publishing Ltd
101 Longden Road, Shrewsbury SY3 9EB, England

DEDICATION

This book is dedicated to my uncle, Victor Hill, who started it all, and my wife Caroline, who puts up with it all.

ACKNOWLEDGEMENTS

Although this book is dedicated to my wife, Caroline, I cannot let the opportunity to acknowledge her help and support pass me by. Late nights agonising over the text, both in draft and edited form, should have driven her crazy, but her patience is legendary and if the book does its task and helps other pigeon shooters to better understand their quarry, then she is as much to thank as anyone.

Ashley Boon, a young wildlife artist with an enormous future, was introduced to me at Chatsworth Country Fair by Phil Pugh of the BASC, and the moment I saw his work I knew that he was the right man to illustrate this book. Ashley is a hunter, with raptors, the rod and the gun and through his love of hunting he brings this passion for wild quarry to the pages of this book. 'A picture is worth a thousand words' is a cliché until you look at the work of the likes of Ashley. My thanks indeed to him for allowing me to share these pages with a talent such as his. My other two collaborators, John Harradine and Chris Cradock, are both friends of long standing, and without them nothing would have been written. Their encouragement to write this book was boundless, and John spent many, many hours playing devil's advocate to some of my more shaky scientific theories. His respect for the woodpigeon is second to none and both he and Dr Nicola Reynolds, also of the BASC, earn my gratitude. Their paper on the woodpigeon is probably the most up-to-date, all-encompassing scientific work available on the subject. Jonathan Young, who was kind enough to write the foreword to this book, is a multi-talented, and very busy man, he is also a friend and I thank him for his time and his erudite words. My thanks, too, to Dr Ian Inglis of MAFF, Dr Steve Smith of the NFU, Dr Mike Swan, and the Game Conservancy Trust for allowing me to share their knowledge; also to many friends, especially Stephen Halstead and Mike Dawnay, who insisted that I wrote the book. On a very personal level I am so greatly indebted to Archie and Prue Coats that words will not do them justice.

I have probably read nearly every author on pigeons and pigeon shooting that is available and I would particularly like to thank John Humphreys and Colin Willock for their words of wisdom over the years. Sadly, my great friend Arthur Sheperd is no longer with us, but Arthur taught me a great deal and we shared many a pigeon hide together. John Darling is without doubt one of the greatest sporting photographers of our time, and a friend; we have shared pigeon hides, duck blinds and many other things over the years. I admire his talent with the camera and I am very happy that he agreed to take the photographs for this book. *Shooting Times* deserve an enormous word of thanks for publishing my articles over the last ten years and so, too, do all the pigeon shooters I have met up and down the country at game fairs, club meetings, pigeon forums and the like.

My thanks must also go to Jean Loubere, his family and all my other friends in France who introduced me to the intricacies of the various *palombières* I have had the privilege to visit over the years. Their knowledge is only matched by their hospitality! Richard Duplock, who produced and directed both videos about the woodpigeon has been patient and kind to me for nearly ten years now and his help on determining the patterns of wing-bar movement has helped my decoying immensely.

Finally, a special word of thanks to Holland & Holland who have allowed me to shoot their guns at woodpigeon for many years. A worthy gun for a worthy target.

Contents

FOREWORD

by Jonathan Young, Editor of *The Field*

The pigeon is the equal of any gamebird and better than most. Take a late-January Home Counties shoot, when a line of moderate shots is industriously shooting mediocre pheasants and the cartridge-to-kill ratio is of a Krupp-like efficiency. On the last drive pigeon start swirling round the hangar wood, a favoured roost. A fusillade goes up, nothing comes down, and no one is much surprised. The pigeon is not only much better than most gamebirds; he's better than most gameshots.

Perhaps that is why the pigeon will always be blackballed in any attempt to join that exclusive club of quarry accorded their own gamebook column. The woodpigeon, in fustian grey, must slum it in 'Various' with crows and other rogues. Of course his reputation is further impaired by his prodigious breeding and feeding. The partridge and grouse are gloriously foppish in their willingness to succumb to any predator or disease. Heavy rain in Ascot Week and that's it for the wild partridges yet again. And food? Well, unless the heather or hedgerow diet is just right the gamebirds simply keel over. Meanwhile the pigeon stuffs his crop and the farmers' too.

Yet despite his plebeian nature, the pigeon has friends in high places, including the best shots in Britain. There are tall-pheasant experts and grouse gurus, but the First XI are both, usually because they practise on pigeon. One day he will be skimming the wheat low, sliding in the wind, the sort of shot that commands a minor fortune on a Yorkshire moor. The next he will be flighting over with a tail wind, forty-five yards up and sixty miles an hour fast, a Dulverton *doppelgänger* in everything but price tag.

Such sporting brilliance is changing our perception of the pigeon. He is still a major agricultural pest, but today there is a growing number of pigeon professionals who will provide a day of superlative sport for the cost of a handful of pheasants. And if you do not have the time to do three days' reconnaissance, access to thousands of acres of arable, a dozen dead birds for decoys, the ability to set them out and build a hide, then a professional guide is a boon. (He will also teach you to shoot.)

John Batley has been a pigeon guide longer than most, Archie Coats' disciple and successor. Like Major Coats, he is an unusual man, an ex-racing mechanic and rally driver, fluent in three languages, who also works for Holland & Holland. He is also a countryman and a long-standing friend, the quality of whose cellar is only exceeded by the loveliness of his wife.

This book contains his distilled wisdom and will be a standard work on the pigeon. For it is not just about how to shoot them but is an appreciation of the bird's remarkable qualities. Too many people think numbers in pigeon shooting: a 100-bird day is good, thirty birds is bad, particularly if the standard of shooting has been ropey. Yet if those birds had been pheasants, part of a 250-bird day where every one accounted for cost five cartridges, would they not be cause for celebration?

Introduction

T
he woodpigeon has enabled me to feed and clothe my family, travel to fascinating places and meet many, many people. It has taught me patience, how to shoot better, and, very importantly, it has shown me how to respect nature and the weather and, hopefully, to be at one with them. I am extremely fond of the woodpigeon.

Since the 1950s, I have been fortunate enough to shoot woodpigeon all over the British Isles and I have done so using many different guns. They range from my first, a single-barrel Belgian .410 folding hammer gun, to a Holland & Holland prototype over and under Royal sidelock. There were times when the 'day job' got in the way, and some years were leaner than others. I think that these two factors made me realise that if something was not done, I would end my days without ever being able to say that I had at least tried to master a career. With this in mind I gave up the 'day job' in 1983 and since early 1984 I have been a professional pigeon shooter.

I do not claim to have reached the heights of the great, and unique, Archie Coats; however, I have learned a great deal, mainly by making mistakes. I have therefore decided it is time I shared some of the experiences and passed on some of the knowledge. My gamebooks have provided me with more than enough information to fill these pages, but you will find little of numbers here as it is not necessary to remember numbers. Remember the quality rather than the quantity.

The book is divided into five sections: What, Where, When, How, and a chapter on the legal and ethical position, and there are two further appendices at the end. The first deals with the issue of non-toxic shot and is by Dr John Harradine, Head of Research at the British Association of Shooting and Conservation (BASC), an admirer, and hunter, of the woodpigeon, and a friend and colleague of many years' standing. The second contains some words of wisdom from Chris Cradock on the subject of shooting, gun fit and woodpigeon. Chris is a dear friend and knows as much about shooting as anyone could hope to know. Apart from anything else, he has spent nearly fifty years of his life teaching people to shoot.

Hand in hand with the hunting of wild quarry should always go the research into the well-being of that quarry. BASC has always been at the forefront of any action to protect the status of a quarry which is under threat, and as a result of the 1990 furore over the proposed closed season for the woodpigeon in Great Britain, a working party was formed to look into various aspects of the bird. I am proud to say that I am one of the founder members of that working party and I fervently hope that our work will result in us all getting to know the bird better.

Fieldcraft today is harder to practise than ever before and the hunt is the thing. The bag, although always welcome, is merely a physical representation of the quality of the fieldcraft applied to those conditions on that particular day. Nature, including the weather, controls wild creatures and the hunting of them.

Woodpigeon (*Columba palumbus*)

1
What

The woodpigeon is one of the great birds of the world. It can fly at up to fifty miles an hour in level flight. It belongs to the only species of birds which sucks water to drink. It feeds its young on 'pigeon milk'. It can stand on its tail and disappear out of view before you can get the gun on it. It can breed up to three times a year. It can be fooled into landing amongst decoys and, above all, it provides accessible shooting to thousands of sportsmen throughout the whole year.

Before we discuss the Where, When and How of pigeon shooting we need to look very carefully at the bird itself in order to better understand our quarry. First of all, it is regarded as the only species of sporting quarry bird which is also classified as an agricultural pest, and one which can be legally shot (by authorised persons) during all months of the year in Great Britain. What is more, it is extremely good to eat. *Columba palumbus* has been with us a very long time indeed – some say millions of years, others only thousands. For all practical purposes it has been present in this country long enough to have established itself as an indigenous bird, and its habits are sufficiently ingrained for us to be able to state them with confidence.

Let us start with the name: *Columba palumbus*, the woodpigeon, the Quist (in Wales), the Doo or Cushie Doo (in Scotland), the Cushat, the ring-necked dove and the woodie. All one and the same bird. It is about sixteen inches long and has a wingspan of just over two feet. The average weight of the adult is about eighteen to twenty ounces.

The colour is predominantly grey, the striking features being the wing bars and the neck ring, both of which are white. The breast is a beautiful shade of pink, turning almost purple as the bird gets older, and the tail has a dark tip, as do the wings. One of its most striking features is the eyes which are bright straw yellow and give the pigeon the appearance of always being on the alert. The legs and feet are reddish, turning darker as the bird gets older, and the wattles on the beak become whiter with age. The sexes are difficult to tell apart but the male is the slightly larger of the two, and has somewhat brighter plumage. The woodpigeon's song is one of the best known of all British countryside sounds in the balmy summer months, and consists of five notes: Coo-cooo-coo, coo-coo.

The courting, or 'cocking', flight is easily recognisable and is only performed by the male. The bird flies in a series of swoops between trees rising and falling quite steeply, and as he rises, he virtually stalls in mid-air and claps his wings before alighting in a tree, hoping that the female will join him. Once in the tree both birds indulge in a bowing display before mating.

The woodpigeon is a prolific breeder, nesting up to three times a year if there is sufficient food available and the weather is warm enough. Two white eggs are laid each time (giving rise to the old saying that twins are a 'pigeon pair'). The breeding season, in the main, runs from the end of

March to the end of October, but eggs have been found in all months of the year. The nest itself is a flimsy affair consisting of a rough platform of twigs which is built anywhere from ten to twenty feet up in trees and hedges; the type of tree seems to make little difference, and they will happily use whatever is available. The incubation period for the eggs is around seventeen to twenty-one days and the birds are fledged at between twenty-eight and thirty-five days. The young are called squabs.

The woodpigeon is unique in that, like other Columbiformes, it does not tip its head back to swallow the water it drinks, but sucks it up, as through a straw, in one continuous draught. It drinks a considerable amount of water, which is important for us, as hunters, to know. I was fortunate enough to spend some time with Archie Coats at the last game fair he attended. On one occasion when he was surrounded, as usual, by a crowd of pigeon shooters, I listened to a young man with yet another question: 'Major Coats, there is laid corn everywhere at the moment and there are pigeon all over the place, but I just can't seem to find where they are feeding.' Quick as a flash, Archie turned to him and said one word: 'Water!' Then he explained that when pigeon are feeding on ripening corn it swells up in their crops and makes them even more thirsty than usual. 'Look for water, my boy, and then look for pigeon flying from that water until you find the field which they are working.' Archie's fieldcraft and grasp of the basic mechanics of the woodpigeon was second to none and he wasted little time trying to overcomplicate life in pigeon terms.

As the birds begin to build nests their hormonal structure changes, and by the time that the eggs are hatched both parents will be producing a type of milk (a cheesy, smelly substance!) on which they will feed the blind nestlings for the first few days of their lives. The feeding process is unlike that of most other birds in that the young, rather than opening their beaks to receive food from their parents, stick their beaks into their parents' gape to feed on the milk, and later, regurgitated vegetable matter. This type of feeding means that the young are virtually force-fed a diet very rich in protein and begs the question as to why this is necessary; after all, most other nestlings are not fed so intensively. My own supposition is that as pigeons form a very large part of many woodland predators' diets, they have a very real need to grow as quickly as possible into fully fledged birds and thus make themselves less of an easy target for their enemies.

The eggs are incubated and the young fed by both parents for the whole time that they remain in the nest. Mother and father take it in turns to feed the 'squeakers' – father during the day, and , as you would expect, mother all night! I think that this will go a long way to dispelling

Adult feeding nestlings

that old myth that, if you shoot a left and right in summer you risk shooting two parents which are feeding young. Like the royal family, pigeon parents rarely risk flying together when they are responsible for youngsters.

Indeed, *Columba palumbus* is a fascinating bird if ever there was one. Not only does it feed its young on milk, it has a number of other features which make it more interesting than your average bird. For example, every chick is hatched with the white wing bars already in place but without the distinctive white neck band seen in the adult. This band – in fact there are two of them, one on each side of the neck – only appears when the bird is old enough to breed. Nature is very direct. The pigeon is a flock bird, and if you are a pigeon wanting to breed, why waste time trying to breed with another member of the flock if that bird is too young to reproduce? The neck band is also used (along with the wing bars), as a flock recognition signal, and I think its use is very closely related to the pigeon's vision. For our purposes, as pigeon shooters, there are two sorts of birds: predators and prey. Woodpigeon are prey, and like every other prey bird they have their eyes set at the sides of their heads. Predators have their eyes in front of their heads. Prey need to see where predators are coming from, both when they are flying and when they are on the ground feeding. Predators, specifically hawks and falcons, attack head into wind and usually from above and behind their prey, which generally also fly head into wind. Prey birds also land and feed on the ground with their heads into the wind.

Woodpigeon, in winter at least, spend most of their waking hours either flying around looking for food or actually on the ground feeding. Their eyesight needs to be exceptionally good. They need to have as much all-round vision as possible, so that they can avoid being taken by surprise while on the ground feeding. In fact a pigeon's eyesight is ideal for its role as a ground feeder. The woodpigeon has 340 degrees of vision. As the bird's eyes are set so far apart on the sides of its head this vision is split up into two distinct areas of monocular vision each covering 170 degrees. Furthermore, it only has a very narrow band of binocular vision, twenty-four degrees to be precise. It has a relatively small blind spot behind it and, by turning its head slightly, it can cover the full 360 degrees quite easily.

I have a theory about pigeons' eyesight on which most of my theory and practice of decoying is based. I believe that pigeons rely, for most of the time, on the broad bands of monocular vision and only use the narrow binocular band when preparing to land, and landing, on branches and the ground. I think it follows that if the bird is concentrating on an area in front of it in binocular vision, then it must be momentarily blind out of this area. On many occasions when I have been decoying in a cross wind I have noticed that, if you stand and try to take the bird too early, it will see you and jink away. If, however, you let the bird come well into the decoys and stand to shoot it when it is only fifteen or twenty yards away, it appears to keep coming in to land as if it had not seen you at all. I believe that this is because the bird has switched to binocular vision in order to land and, when it does so, it is temporarily blind to the sides. Based on this observation I have rearranged my decoy patterns over the years so that the approach into the pattern is as uncluttered as possible. I think that this uncluttered approach allows the bird to commit itself to landing earlier than in a pattern where there are groups of decoys placed almost at random, thus causing the bird to switch constantly from binocular to monocular vision and back again in order to land easily.

When a pigeon is on the ground feeding, it uses monocular vision most of the time to keep an eye on its companions on either side. A feeding pigeon's head bobs up and down almost constantly and the white neck bands move with the head. The moment one of the birds senses danger the head stops moving and remains upright; this is clearly visible to its companions on either side because of the changed position of the neck band. Within moments the whole flock have their heads up, and they take off for safer pastures as one. How the young birds with no neck bands fit into this explanation I have not yet quite worked out! There is no doubt in my mind, however, that the white wing bars and neck bands serve a very useful purpose in the pigeon world: not only do they use them for flock recognition purposes but also for warning each other of impending danger. These white markings are common in nature – rabbit and fallow deer tails are but two examples.

Woodpigeons' hearing seems to have little significance for us as hunters. Their hearing is keen, but it would seem that the sound of a human voice in a hide means nothing to them. They are much more alert to seen, rather than heard, signals of danger. A quick movement of hands and face over the top of a net will frighten them, a cough will not. In France there is a long established form of hunting migratory pigeon which, amongst other things, involves calling to pigeons in trees in order to persuade them to leave their perches and come down to the ground where they may be netted. This is very effective but it should be remembered that pigeons only call whilst perched in trees and not when on the ground or when flying. The idea of calling pigeon in a similar way to duck or geese is a non-starter. Pigeons also have senses of smell, taste and touch, but there is little doubt that of the five senses, vision is by far and away the most important.

We shall be dealing with the pigeon's diet in each month of the year later on in the book, but let us for the moment have a look at its general eating habits. Woodpigeons, contrary to popular belief, are omnivorous. They are mainly seed and weed eaters but will happily eat slugs and snails if there is nothing else around. Pigeons are surface feeders; they do not dig for their food like most other birds. I have yet to see a woodpigeon with a worm in its crop. Their beaks are designed to tear leaves and pick up things like grain, acorns and beech mast, but not to dig.

What they eat is stored in their crops before being digested, which gives them enormous advantages over many other creatures. In winter, for example, they can fill up their crops with half a day's ration of food in the afternoon and then go to roost knowing that they can slowly digest that food over the cold hours of darkness, and survive all but the lowest temperatures. The crop, by virtue of its size, means that the pigeon can survive on many foods of very low nutritional value. It can store more food at any one time, in relation to its overall body weight, than most of its avian cousins, giving it a better chance of survival over the winter months when there is not much nutritious food to be found. Oilseed rape leaves are a perfect example of this storing of food of low calorific value. In winter a pigeon eats up to twenty-five per cent of its total body weight every day. Instances of pigeons being shot on their way home to roost with as many as twenty-five acorns in their crops are not uncommon. Their metabolic rate is quite high, but their conversion of food into energy is inefficient. Let us look at a few facts. If a pigeon weighs twenty ounces and, on average over the whole year, it eats fifteen per cent of its own body weight every day, it will consume over sixty-eight pounds of food every year. Twelve thousand birds will eat a ton every day! In 1965, Dr R. K. Murton of the Ministry of Agriculture, Fisheries and Food estimated the pigeon population at around ten million birds. This means that pigeons eat around 833 tons every day, just over three hundred thousand tons a year! No wonder the woodpigeon is classed as Britain's major bird pest. A thousand birds can eat up to one ton in a week during the winter months, and a single pigeon can eat enough wheat grains in a week to make a two-pound loaf of bread.

Having said that the pigeon population was estimated at ten million thirty years ago, we should now look at more modern estimates and see how they affect our hunting of the species today. The bad news is that there are no more modern estimates than those of Murton and his colleagues. The good news is that the BASC and the Game Conservancy Trust are presently conducting a joint research programme, funded by the Duke of Westminster Trust, which will eventually give us a better insight into population figures today. This research, in which I am involved, will be based on bag studies and ringing data and will hopefully include help from the British Trust for Ornithology (BTO), Joint Nature Conservation Committee (JNCC), Ministry of Agriculture, National Farmers Union (NFU) and other bodies. The BASC started their long-term programme of bag counts in 1993.

In the absence of official estimates, much speculation abounds as to the total woodpigeon population of the United Kingdom, ranging from the view of Dr Inglis of the Ministry of Agriculture that the figure has not much changed from Murton's time, to my own view, that with the enormous increase in the acreage of winter oilseed rape the population is rising steadily, and has probably reached seventeen or eighteen million. It must be said that Dr Inglis' conclusion is drawn from continued research at Carlton (the Ministry of Agriculture's site in Cambridgeshire) where the agricultural pattern has changed greatly over the years; and, as Dr Inglis freely admits, his figures are restricted solely to one small area of the whole country, and my own 'guesstimate' is drawn purely from my experience of pigeon watching over the years. Whatever the true figure, I am sure that we shall all benefit from the results of the research, one of which will be how many birds are shot every year. At present the figure seems to fluctuate wildly. I hear numbers ranging from two to ten million being quoted with gay abandon! My own 'guesstimate' is around six million annually, but of course I could be wrong.

One of the other great debates in the woodpigeon world is that of migration. This subject is discussed endlessly wherever a few pigeon shooters are gathered over a beer or two. Dr Murton, in whom I had great faith, was of the opinion that the British woodpigeon was, in the main, sedentary. I wholeheartedly agree with him for the following reasons: the scientific evidence from returns of ringed birds shows that only a few birds migrate; and if migration did take place, this would happen in late October or early November. There is no evidence of this.

The prime motivation for any species of bird to migrate is to keep alive during the harsh winter months by flying south to warmer and less hostile climes. In mainland Europe where the winters are still much colder than ours, the feeding grounds are very often snow-covered from late October to mid-March and the majority of woodpigeons are still migratory. Amongst other things, my own reasons for believing that our pigeon do not migrate include the fact that I have shot at migratory pigeons in both Sweden and France, and I can assure you that they behave very differently from our own English variety! I have never encountered birds as skittish as those that are migrating, or about to migrate. They approach the decoys, and are gone again in a flash. More often than not, they do not even come within range of the gun. As far as birds migrating *into* the UK are concerned, I would merely point out that the main migratory routes south from northern Europe pass well to the east of the British Isles.

There are other more interesting and important factors than migration which concern pigeon shooters today. By 1976 farmers were being subsidised to grow winter oilseed rape in such quantities that the pigeon, used to a fairly scarce food supply in winter, were able to pick and choose where they fed to an extent that they never had before. Until then most farmers had harvested their crops in late summer and left the majority of their fields bare until the traditional spring planting. Pigeons had a hard time finding food in winter on the bare plough and the sparse acreage of winter wheat and were obliged to seek food on the clover leys and in the woods. It is no accident that Archie Coats (in January 1962) took his record bag of 550 birds in a day on clover. That was all that was available to the birds. Clover was nutritious, and still is, but now there are many more acres of oilseed rape than clover and the fields are easier to strip bare.

If the 1970s saw the demise of the old ways of winter pigeon decoying it also saw the start of what has become the curse of all contemporary pigeon shooters: the winter pigeon flock and 'rape' pigeons. In the old days pigeons would stay in relatively small flocks in any one place over the winter for the simple reason that there was not enough food to sustain a flock of several thousand birds. That has all changed with the advent of winter oilseed rape. We have nearly a million acres of it today and it is not uncommon to see a flock of 3,000 or more birds on a block of 200 acres.

Pigeons flock up at the onset of winter. In the UK this is usually around the second week of December (a little earlier in Scotland). I believe that the process of flocking is governed by the amount of daylight available. I have been told that the pineal gland, which measures light, will determine the moment of flocking. The reason why the birds flock in the short cold days of winter is their need to

357,480

spend most of the ever-decreasing daylight hours on the ground looking for, and eating, food. Obviously the more time pigeon spend on the ground, the more at risk each is to attack by a predator. It therefore follows that the more of them there are together, the less chance each has of being the one to get picked off by a hawk. It further follows that if 200 acres of rape can be found fairly near to hand, the pigeon are in clover, so to speak, with an abundant supply of food to keep them going all winter.

Sadly for the pigeon shooter, pigeons which are in a flock tend to move as a flock. This makes decoying a very difficult task. It is much easier to decoy pigeons which move either singly or in small groups of less than a dozen. In 'How' we shall be looking at decoying rape pigeons, but it is only fair to warn you now that it is a very difficult, and sometimes unrewarding, task.

Before we move on to how to hunt these extraordinary birds we must look very carefully at the one thing which governs the behaviour of the woodpigeon more than anything else: the weather. I said in the Introduction that nature and the weather control wild creatures and the hunting of them. This is true, but in fact nature and the weather are virtually one. Nature, if you like, determines the time when wild creatures breed. But if at that time the weather is awful, those same creatures won't breed until the weather gets better.

A pigeon's job in life, as with any creature, is to continue the species. He does this in the only way he knows how, by breeding young and bringing them up to do the same thing. To do this job he has both help and hindrance from nature. Nature provides him with food to sustain him, and nature provides him with enemies to destroy him if he is not careful. The weather describes for the pigeon, on a daily basis, the parameters within which he may operate. On a cold, sunny and windless day you will find your pigeon sitting in a tree, facing south, taking in the warmth of the sun and not flying very much. He will expend little energy and any food he eats will probably be gleaned from an area very close to the tree in which he is perched. On the other hand, imagine a day of blustery showers in early April. Our same pigeon will be seen zipping around his patch, revelling in the wind, which makes flying both easy and a pleasure. He will join his fellow birds in attacking a freshly drilled field of peas or beans and be on the go from dawn to dusk. Why? What is the difference from one day to the next?

To answer this question I will indulge in one of my favourite analogies. Forget about pigeons for the moment and think about desert islands. I am going to abandon you on a small desert island, a few miles off the west coast of Scotland, for a whole week. The time of year is late June. You will be completely on your own, but I will furnish you with some basic survival needs: a tarpaulin, a fishing line and hooks, a knife, a bill-hook, some string, snares, a first-aid kit and a blanket. The island is friendly; there is plenty of water, rabbits abound, there are trout in the streams, there is plenty of firewood and there are wild strawberries. The beaches are sandy and beautiful.

On the day that I drop you off on your island I leave you with enough sandwiches for you not to have to bother to search for your food on your first day on your own. The weather is glorious, the sun is shining, God is in His heaven and all is right with the world. In all probability you will not bother to make a shelter for yourself on that first night. You will probably light a fire on the beach and spend the night under your tarpaulin. After all, you looked at the starlit sky before you settled down and, as it was so clear, you decided that it would be a fine day tomorrow. The next day dawns and, sure enough, you were right – it is another fabulous June day, with sunshine, no clouds and a clear blue sky. You spend the day alternately picking wild strawberries and lounging around on the beach sunbathing. After all, you have nowhere to go, nothing special to do, and the weather looks set to be fine for a long while to come. That night you again look up at the sky and, seeing it clear, you sleep once again under your tarpaulin, without bothering to build yourself a more permanent shelter. The next day dawns clear again, and the next, and the next. By now you are getting a tan and becoming progressively more lazy as the days go on.

After five days and nights on the island you are becoming complacent. What could possibly go wrong? But on the afternoon of the sixth day, at around five o'clock, the sky suddenly goes dark, the rain comes down in sheets and thunder and lightning herald the arrival of the grandaddy of all storms. Needless to say, you panic, and start dashing around trying to do the things that you haven't done all week. You have built no shelter, you have collected no store of either drinking water or food and you probably have very little dry firewood ready for emergencies.

I hope you will agree that this is what would happen to you; I am sure it would happen to me. What we now have to look at is what made us panic. There was no indication of how long the storm would last; it was June, remember? Why were we suddenly dashing about trying to collect food and water and build a shelter? I believe the answer lies in the uncertainty of the situation we were put in without any warning. In short, the weather changed and as we were not ready for the change we panicked and reverted to a much wilder state than the one in which we usually live. In a wild state, when we are threatened by the unknown, we react by looking for the things that mean our very survival, in this case food, water and shelter. Pigeons, of course, live in a permanently wild state, but when they are threatened by a sudden and violent change in the weather, their first reaction seems to be to look for food so that they can face the night with a full crop. Remember that they are not sure what the morrow will bring and when they will be able to feed again.

Back on our island, all that really happened was a sudden drop in barometric pressure, resulting in a storm. Pigeons seem to react to a sudden drop in pressure by feeding more intensively than usual. Interestingly enough there is a parallel to this scenario in the fishing adage, 'When the wind is in the east, the fish bite the least. When the wind is in the west, the fish bite the best.' The weather from the east in this country usually means high pressure, and the weather from the west usually means low pressure. I believe that when the weather is settled (high pressure), pigeons tend to browse rather than feed hard and when the weather is unsettled (low pressure), the birds also become unsettled and feed much harder, thus making them more likely to come to decoys. Barometric pressure is measured in either millibars or inches, and I personally consider that a reading of under 1,000 millibars (29.5 inches) constitutes low pressure in pigeon shooting terms. If the barometer is as high as 1,015 or more, I never expect to shoot a large bag.

I first began to think about these changes in pressure back in 1984–5, my first winter as a professional pigeon shooter. For the first time in my pigeon shooting career I was going out every day and not when *I* thought the weather was right. I began to wonder why I could get a good day followed by a bad day on virtually the same fields and crops. The only answer seemed to be the different weather conditions and I began to keep records of changes in the weather on a daily basis (including rises and falls in barometric pressure). It very soon became obvious that the atmospheric pressure had a lot to answer for and I began to formulate the ideas which I now work to on a regular basis. My best pigeon shooting days have (nearly) always been ones when the barometer was falling, the west wind was blowing hard and the weather was generally unsettled.

Luckily, this formula does not work all the time. Life would be very boring if we could predict with accuracy what wild creatures were going to do before they did it. I firmly believe that there are many other factors which affect a pigeon's willingness to come to decoys: snow, thunderstorms, the cycles of the moon, and many more I probably haven't even thought of!

Stock Dove (*Columba oenas*)

In the modern age in which we live we find ourselves soft and far removed from the hunter-gatherers that we once were. Central heating, cars, freezers and all the other trappings of modern life have robbed us of the oneness with nature that we used to have. Ask any gamekeeper, stalker or ghillie what the weather will be like tomorrow, and he will probably look at the wild creatures in his own environment before attempting to answer your question. In short it behoves us, as hunters of

Rock Dove (*Columba livia*)

wild quarry, to study that quarry before hunting it. The woodpigeon has survived by adapting itself, very successfully, to the environment to which it belongs. To hunt the pigeon we need to understand its environment and fit in to it as best we can.

Let us look at some of the other pigeons and doves we are likely to come across, some of which we may shoot, others not. First of all the stock dove (*Columba oenas*). This is one we may not shoot, as it is protected under the Wildlife and Countryside Act of 1981. I would say

Feral Pigeon (*Columba livia*)

that the stock dove is the cause of more bad language in a pigeon hide than anything else (including bad shooting!). The reason is quite simple: it looks, superficially, like a woodpigeon, flies with woodpigeon and comes even more readily to decoys than a woodpigeon.

The stock dove is, however, smaller than the woodpigeon, roughly thirteen inches long, and weighing several ounces less. Its wing beats are also faster than the woodpigeon's. It is generally a dumpier bird than the woodpigeon and, with a little experience, quite easy to distinguish from its larger cousin. Perhaps the biggest difference between these two birds is the absence of white wing bars and white neck bands in the stock dove. Quite simply, if you see no trace of white wing bars . . . don't shoot. The stock dove is a darker grey than the woodpigeon and there are strong dark green markings on the neck, the breast is mauve and there are black bars visible on the wings, when folded. These birds commonly fly in pairs, and it is said that they pair for life.

One final point about the stock dove that we need to mention here is that this is the bird which is commonly referred to as the 'blue rock'. In reality, blue rock is a mixture of names (most likely referring to the bird which used to be shot in live pigeon shooting from traps at the beginning of the century), and I can find no reference to such a bird in my modern bird books.

Columba livia, the rock dove, is another protected species and these days is rarely found outside the western coasts of Scotland and Ireland where it lives and nests in rocky sea-cliffs. It is roughly of the same size and appearance as the stock dove, but slightly lighter in colour overall. It has two black wing bars and a very noticeable white rump. The problem with *Columba livia* is that all feral and town pigeons are originally descended from it, and are therefore also called *Columba livia*, and this produces an anomaly in the 1981 Wildlife and Countryside Act in that the true rock dove is a protected species and the feral pigeon is not.

Feral pigeons come in different shapes, sizes and colours and really are a pain. If asked to shoot them by your farmer friends, please do so; they come well to decoys but are used to men and really offer very little sport. When feeding on farmland they attract woodpigeons to them, but shooting them can only be seen as a pure crop protection exercise.

A word of warning: racing pigeons are obviously protected birds, and are always ringed, but some of these birds can turn feral and feed with others on farmland. A flock of racing pigeons on the wing is easy to spot

Collared Dove (*Streptopelia decaocto*)

Turtle Dove (*Streptopelia turtur*)

– they are smaller than woodpigeon, fly much faster and, above all, stick together in a flock. It is extremely rare for them to stop in their flight home and come to decoys. A single racing pigeon which has gone feral and left its flock to join other ferals, on the other hand, is very difficult to spot. It is illegal to shoot racing pigeons.

There are two other species which you are likely to see from time to time when out decoying and these are the collared dove and the turtle dove. The collared dove (*Streptopelia decaocto*) is not protected and you may shoot it all the year round. This dove is much smaller than the woodpigeon, being under eleven inches long, and is very different in colouring. In particular it has a narrow, dark brown collar and is generally light brown on the body, rather than grey. It is now sedentary in Britain and is mainly found in small flocks in and around farm buildings and grain stores. It is not difficult to shoot and half a dozen

A.S.

Peregrine falcon with Woodpigeon

make a good meal! The turtle dove (*Streptopelia turtur*), on the other hand, is a migrant and a protected bird. It is roughly the same size as the collared dove but much darker brown in colouring and the neck has distinctive white patches with black stripes. It has very striking eyes which are dark red in colour and its tail is tipped with white.

There is a great deal more that one could say about pigeons, and although we shall be looking in more detail at their feeding patterns and susceptibility to weather conditions, this is intended as a book for the pigeon shooter and not the scientist. There are many learned papers on the subject of *Columba palumbus* and the other species, and if you want further information you should turn to the works of people like Murton, Inglis, Colquhoun, Harradine and others. Dr Murton, who worked for the Ministry of Agriculture, is without doubt the most prolific and widely respected of all who have written on the subject of the woodpigeon and his work is being very ably carried on by Dr Ian Inglis, also of the Ministry of Agriculture.

2
Where

Having established the general habits of the woodpigeon, the next thing we need to know is where to find it. On the face of it this may seem fairly easy.

Woodpigeons are found on fields and in woods. That is all very well, but where are these fields and woods, and why are some fields completely devoid of all pigeon life? And, just as important, how do we get permission to shoot over those fields and in those woods once we have found them?

Let us start with 'where' geographically. We know our agricultural patterns have changed over the last three decades. There is much more land under the plough than ever before and therefore the opportunities for pigeon are much greater.

You can see the main arable areas quite clearly from the map and this is generally where you would expect to find woodpigeon. Our present system of intensive arable farming with subsidies on many crops suits both the farmer and the pigeon. For example, there were a million acres of winter oilseed rape grown in 1991. The total agricultural acreage of Scotland, England and Wales is over forty-three million acres, so you can see that the pigeon is not going to run short of food in the near future! Put another way, if the total population, is say, seventeen million birds, there is one pigeon for every 2.5 acres (or one for every two and a half football pitches).

As a rule of thumb, I would say that I would expect to find pigeon in almost any arable area, especially if it included woods as well as fields.

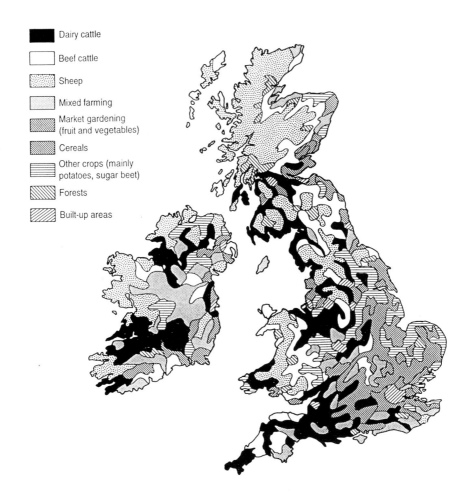

Dairy cattle

Beef cattle

Sheep

Mixed farming

Market gardening
(fruit and vegetables)

Cereals

Other crops (mainly
potatoes, sugar beet)

Forests

Built-up areas

More specifically, I would look for a warm, well-wooded, well-watered environment which offered as much food and seclusion as the pigeon needed, the more rural the better. It is no accident that some of the highest concentrations of pigeon are to be found in the north-east of Scotland and on some of the great private shooting estates of the south and east of England. Food and privacy; a great combination for *Columba palumbus*.

Let's get even more specific. Which are the best fields and woods in which to look for our quarry? The answer will depend on how our farmer grows his crops, what time of year he plants them and what his crop rotation is. All farmers are governed by some kind of crop rotation or other. The reasons are straightforward: if you continue to grow the same crop in the same field year after year you run the risk of disease in the crops and you can starve the earth of its basic nutrients such as nitrates and phosphates. So, you may grow wheat one year, legumes the next, potatoes the next and so on. The system has been going on for generations and works well.

There can be problems for the pigeon shooter, however. On one farm where I have shot pigeons for at least ten years, the farm manager worked very sensibly on a five-year rotation. It was a model farm with no disease and excellent yields, until one year oilseed rape prices went sky high and it was decided to grow rape two years running in the same fields. Result – a ghastly disease (the name of which I can't even pronounce) struck the rape and the yield was halved. So no more rape was grown for two years on that farm. As if by magic the pigeon disappeared. With no winter rape, they had no food to get them through the cold months and they were gone to pastures new. Two years have now passed, the ground has recovered from its sickness, the farm is back into winter rape again and I am shooting pigeon there once more – there are over 1,500 resident there as I write. Interestingly enough, the same exodus of pigeon occurred at the Ministry of Agriculture's control site in Cambridgeshire. When rape went out of the rotation for a year, the pigeons flew off and only returned when winter rape came back into the rotation.

If you think that these examples are unusual, then think again. I have reports of the same sort of thing happening all over the country over the last five years, and it affects between sixty and eighty per cent of the population of the sites involved. The figures for the example on the farm that I shoot are: normal year with winter oilseed rape – average bag p.a. 450–600; two-year break with no winter oilseed rape – average bag p.a. 50–100. Dr Murton was of the opinion that the pigeon population was mainly governed by the amount of winter food available and I agree with him. Conditions are very different today from his era (the 1960s) however, and I think that the pigeon move locally to readily available alternative food sources rather than starve as they often did in his day. So crop rotation is a major element in the 'Where' scenario and not one which can be ignored. Any pigeon shooter worth his salt should have some agricultural knowledge and use it to his advantage. (Later on, in the chapter on 'How', I shall go into other details on woods and water and how they affect the pigeon, but for now, let us continue to review the question of 'Where'.)

Woodpigeon need food, water and shelter and you will generally find them where these three things are in close proximity. Having discovered where the birds are, you need permission to shoot over the land you have found, turning 'the' birds into 'your' birds. What is needed is tact and understanding. We all like talking about ourselves and what we know most about and farmers are no different. In fact, as they tend to be a fairly solitary group of people by virtue of their occupation, they tend to talk more than most, once given the opportunity and asked the right questions.

Imagine the scene. You arrive at a farm unknown to you where you have seen pigeons feeding on a field of winter rape. (This you've seen from the road as you drove past.) 'Good morning,' you say, 'I see you've got pigeons feeding on your rape. May I go and have a shot or two at them?' Answer – yes or no. Unlikely to be yes – he doesn't know you from Adam and you've caught him on market day and he's worried about the price of cattle/lambs/fencing posts or some other of the myriad things that constantly worry farmers. End of conversation and you go away, pigeonless and probably with a flea in your ear for disturbing him.

Try another approach. 'Good morning. I see you've got pigeon on the rape and from what I could see from the road, you've got about 100 acres. Do they do much damage? Do they stay on into spring and take anything off the other 400 acres you farm?' Answer: 'How do you know that I've got 500 acres to farm you cheeky young thing?' 'Well sir, I always thought that farms were worked in a five-year rotation and I calculated that the fields that I saw were about 100 acres, so . . .' You have now provoked a conversation (by what the salesmen call an open question) and if you are not daft, the subject of pigeon shooting can be brought up before long. It may not be Booker Prize-winning dialogue but it's a hundred times better than the direct approach which usually invites a straightforward no. (As an easy guide, an acre is about seventy paces by seventy paces, and in EU terminology, one hectare = 2.47 acres.)

Whilst we're on the subject, let us look more closely at getting permission to shoot pigeons on land which doesn't belong to us and/or is not rented by us. A farm is like a large back garden. Would you like it if some scruffy oik trampled all over your borders and your lawn and dropped litter all over the place? Of course not, and the farmer is no different. He just has a much bigger garden, that's all. He also almost always has fields that border roads so he is permanently up to his ears in litter before you even arrive to desecrate his garden further.

As a cardinal rule, I never try to approach a farmer for the first time unless I am properly dressed: cords, tie, waistcoat, etc. and above all no gun, no camouflage and no pigeon shooting gear in obvious evidence in

the vehicle. Nowadays, it is easier and I can give references. But I had to start off in virgin territory like anybody else and it was often a question of waiting hours to see the man for about five minutes of his time. Mornings are usually best; elevenish as a general rule of thumb seems to work for me. Harvest is not a good time. Winter is; fewer things going on in the farm means more time to talk to you.

Once I have spoken with a farmer who doesn't throw me out straight away, I always write to him (to thank him for his time if nothing else) and offer personal details like car make, colour and registration number, BASC membership number and shotgun certificate number. Farmers are not fools nor do they live in the Dark Ages, and prospective pigeon shooters must go about the job of getting permission to shoot in a serious and professional way.

Other ways of getting permission, apart from 'cold calling', include having a friend invite you or recommend you, buying a day or a lease, or going out with a professional pigeon guide. Or you can join the BASC (which you should do anyway), and apply for membership of your local pigeon club. It is much harder to get permission than it was ten years ago, but the pigeon is still a pest and there are still farmers willing to let you have some free sport in return for some genuine crop protection.

To summarise, here is a list of dos and don'ts for getting and maintaining approval:

1. Always turn up at the farm armed with the farmer's name.
2. Don't hassle him at inconvenient times, e.g. milking.
3. Present yourself correctly dressed – no camouflage gear, etc.
4. Offer details and references about yourself, BASC membership, etc.
5. Have some idea of the size of the farm.
6. If given permission to shoot, ask for a map of the farm (all farmers have them) and ask for a tour of the farm, if the farmer has time.
7. If you get permission, write and confirm details.
8. Once you are there, DON'T LEAVE LITTER – NOTHING, NOTHING, NOTHING!
9. Don't hack down hedges, especially ones containing hardwoods.
10. Don't drive on the fields without express permission.
11. Don't park anywhere on the farm where you will impede the farmer's work.
12. Know the public rights of way on the farm.
13. Keep an eye out for wandering stock or broken gates and either tell the farmer about it or fix it yourself.
14. Offer pigeons or other game to the farmer and his family.
15. Treat the farm and the farmer as you would your own home, garden and family.
16. Let the farmer know when you are coming in advance; phone the night before. If you don't see him when you get to the farm, leave a note for him (the 'post-it' type), on his back door or inside your windscreen.
17. Carry your shotgun certificate with you in the car when you go shooting.
18. If game is shot on the farm, make sure you know the dates and offer to go beating on those days.
19. Don't take along a friend unless you have permission to do so.
20. Once again, NO LITTER!

Now, let me tell you a couple of stories which illustrate some of the points I've been making. The first concerns a little old lady who was on her way to church at 9.30 one Sunday morning. She lived in a very small market town not far from where we live, which had one set of traffic lights halfway along the main street. Our little old lady approached the traffic lights, head bowed against the blustery weather, pushed the button at the lights and waited for the signal to cross. Along came a car, slowed and stopped for the lights and the lady, raising her head slightly, saw a car full of men dressed in camouflage gear including caps and what looked like guns on the rear parcel shelf. She was not to know that it was merely four chaps off pigeon shooting. She had seen an item on the TV news the night before about terrorists and so phoned the police. The pigeon shooters took nearly two hours to extricate themselves from police custody and the story goes (locally) that, confronted with so many armed police, they had to change their camouflage garments before leaving, and in fact left most of them, especially the trousers, with the police. They will never again put on their camouflage coats until they are actually in their hides!

A second story comes to mind. One very cold, snowy Sunday morning I was walking a field of rape to keep the pigeons off the crop when, halfway back to the road, I saw a couple of people approaching me through the snow – two young men in camouflage gear, one with a closed gun under his arm, the other with a dog at his heel. They stopped and said, 'Any chance of some pigeon shooting, mate?' They had seen my vehicle and recognised it, and had thought they might 'do a bit of pigeon shooting'. This just goes to show how daft some people can be. These young men were committing a legal offence called armed trespass, and it could have had fairly major consequences if they had been taken to court.

3
When

T he life of a pigeon shooter is one of relative ease. We don't have to trudge over miles of heather for our quarry nor do we have to spend hours up to our ears in mud as do our wildfowling cousins. We are only out in daylight and, once we have got the system worked out, we spend most of our time sitting down. Yes, we spend hours and hours driving around during reconnaissance, but again, this is during the day and we are warm and dry in our vehicles.

Woodpigeon are early risers – they are usually up and about soon after dawn – and they are fairly early to bed at around dusk. If you are standing hopefully in a roosting wood waiting for pigeon to come in with darkness falling and the rooks, jackdaws and crows are cackling away on their way to roost, and nothing has happened, you know that the pigeon have eluded you that day and are already in bed somewhere else. The blackbirds are always later to roost than the pigeon.

So what is the best time for the pigeon shooter? In my youth the word was that you needed to have your hide and decoys set up before dawn and that your best shooting was always in the winter. This has all changed. Nowadays the majority of decent shooting takes place after midday and the best bags seem to be had in the spring and summer. There are several reasons for the changes. Firstly, the advances of agricultural science have provided more and more varied crops for the pigeon to eat and they are no longer under such severe pressure, particularly in the winter, to feed on the one field in thirty or forty that held clover. Secondly, the winters, certainly over the last ten years, have hardly been severe. (If you think this is not so, think back, if you can, to the winters of 1947 and 1963.) The pigeons' choices are wider, life is softer and I think that they tend to feed in different patterns than in the 1950s.

The daily pattern seems to run rather like this: get up at dawn, dash off down the flight line to a suitable field to feed for up to one and a half hours, retire to the trees, either individually or in groups, sit in the sun, preen the feathers, have a quiet nap, digest the food and then perhaps at around eleven o'clock in the morning continue flying around, being nosy and seeing what your friends are up to. Around lunchtime (human time), you could drop into a field or hedgerow for a light snack perhaps (the equivalent of hamburger and chips). Then retire to the trees again and wait for mid- to late afternoon and then get seriously stuck into the feed again to last you through the night. This pattern is followed winter, spring, summer and autumn.

As you would expect, there are variations on the theme. Pigeons are great survivors and if, for example, it is raining non-stop for two or three days, the birds will probably feed little on the first day or day and a half and then appear to feed permanently for the next day and a half. This is normal behaviour if you want to survive. What we must always remember is that what I am writing here are guidelines, not absolute hard and fast rules.

Thirty years ago, the pigeon seemed to eat three meals a day – breakfast, lunch and supper – and you knew where to find him at any given time. Nowadays, the greater availability of palatable food and the increased shooting pressure seems to have changed his eating habits and I am of the belief that he is now more likely to eat (and then digest) as and when he can. Imagine driving from London to Scotland for the first time and not knowing where the filling stations are, nor the hours that they are open. You could fill the car in London, drive 300 miles and then hope to find a garage, but, if you were more sensible, you would top up the tank every 100 miles or so and rest easy in your mind, knowing that you would never run out of petrol. Similarly, I think that with the amount of disturbance and shooting the average pigeon encounters, he is more likely to feed in short, sharp bursts, never quite emptying his system, rather than taking the longer, more leisurely meals of times gone past. Another important point to bear in mind, I think, is that if you disturb him at what I consider to be his most important meal of the day, his breakfast, you will run the risk of him flying off never to be seen again for the rest of the day.

Pigeons are creatures of habit and they normally remain in the same areas all their lives, flying around them every day. If you disturb them when they are desperate to feed early in the morning, you may get between one and one and a half hours' shooting but, as they really need to pack in the calories, they will be off to the other end of their patch and you will not see them again all day. It is better to do your reconnaissance in the morning and watch where they go after breakfast.

Why should breakfast be his most important meal of the day? There are several reasons. Firstly, you never know what is going to happen to you later in the day in the way of disturbance, so start the day with plenty of food in your crop. Secondly it may have been a cold night, in which case you need the kick-start of food to get you through to the warmer part of the day. Thirdly, dawn is the most undisturbed time of the day in the country. There are fewer people around and you can probably feed more in a more leisurely way than at any other time of the day. Over the last ten years or so, I have taken more and more to shooting in the afternoons and my biggest bags in that time have all been made after lunch.

The next thing to consider is the best time of year for shooting. First we must answer a moral question. Should we shoot during the breeding season or not? The problem, as we have seen, is that the pigeon has been known to breed in every month of the year, so that causes a dilemma.

I look at the matter in a different way, with different questions. Does the law allow me to shoot all the year round? At the moment, yes. Is the pigeon population declining under the present laws? No. Are there sufficient pigeons in my area to warrant year-round shooting? At the present time, yes. I therefore look at it from a hunter's point of view, and if I know my area through experience and fieldcraft, and I know that the population is rising or stable, then I have no compunction about shooting in every month of the year. However, I will not take commercial clients shooting during the early summer months, especially over laid corn, where the risk of losing birds is high. This brings me neatly to my fourth reason for shooting twelve months of the year: crop protection. The woodpigeon, like it or not, is registered as an agricultural pest and we have the right to control it, whether it is the breeding season or not. I see it not as a moral issue but merely as a question of necessity. In the end you must make up your own mind. I merely offer suggestions to help you see the issue objectively rather than emotionally. At the moment, I am satisfied with my reasons and I shoot all year round. If I wish to change that, then it should be my decision, taken freely as a hunter and not imposed on me by others, be they politicians or members of the anti-shooting lobby.

But what is the *best* time of the year? I have already said that thirty years ago it used to be winter. Now it has changed, and I believe that the reason is the availability of food. During the winter months, when the

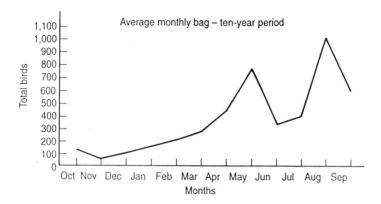

pigeon don't want to travel very far because of the nasty weather and the lack of daylight hours, they will all go to the nearest available food supply. That is why many of the huge bags used to be taken in winter: the birds only had a very limited number of fields on which they *had* to feed in order to survive. The canny decoyer knew his ground and it was simply a question of which field they were on and, 'let's get set up and start shooting.'

Now it is a completely different world. There are winter crops everywhere, especially winter oilseed rape, nearly a million acres of it, all over the place, even in the far south-west where thirty years ago there was only grass for cattle. There are fat subsidies for growing arable winter crops. No wonder the decoyer does badly and the pigeon thrives. The birds are no longer limited to a few fields for their survival. If they hear a few shots they can move, as a flock, to pastures new, leaving the shooter to chase them all day from one field to the next – a very unprofitable pastime!

Pigeons, like many other flock birds, flock up when the hours of daylight shrink to the point where they must be on the ground feeding nearly all of the time available to them. They flock to reduce their chances of being caught by predators, and when they move, they move as a flock. This flock will stay together all winter and not break up until the spring; usually late March. If you look at the graph showing the results of my shooting over the last ten years or so, you will see that the high points are in spring and summer and most of the low points are in winter.

My year starts in October, so let us look at a whole year's shooting starting from then.

OCTOBER

Most of the harvest is in by now, a large proportion of winter crops are being drilled, the rest of the ground is being worked down, and there is little stubble left apart from that which is being designated as set-aside. The beech mast and acorns are not quite ready to provide a staple diet. So, with the breeding season just about over and the birds not yet in flocks for the winter, where will they be? And what will they be feeding on?

If it is warm, they will browse, flitting from wood to field to wood. There is no urgency, the family is fledged, you're fit and well and there's plenty of sunshine and the days are still relatively long. A little chick-weed for starters, perhaps? Followed by some spilt wheat grains and then on to an acorn or two or, if you're really lucky, your farmer has some beans still to harvest and they will spill out of the pod and be lying conveniently on the ground. If it is windy, on the other hand, how about whizzing off to that far field of freshly drilled winter wheat? There are plenty of options but, in general, they don't seem to concentrate on any particular patch for a long time.

NOVEMBER

In my experience, this is usually a cold, wet, miserable month and the pigeons, in my area at least, seem to spend most of their time in the woods keeping dry. It is consistently my worst month for a decent day's shooting and I suspect it is because the birds tend to stay close to the wood, living mainly on berries, the remains of the elder, hips, haws, acorns, beech mast and the like. Plenty of nutrition without much effort. Stay at home, keep dry and keep your head down. Another minus, I am afraid, despite the birds' eagerness not to venture too far from the trees, is that there is still plenty of leaf left on the trees and it is therefore too early in the winter to start roost shooting. Oh well, roll on spring!

DECEMBER

This is the month of one of the big biological changes. The birds flock up, usually in the first fifteen days of the month, and they will stay in a flock until March. Their diet? Well, mainly the leaves of the winter sown oilseed rape; there is enough of it to see them right through the winter and they will, if possible, stay on the same patch all winter long. Obviously they will eat other things such as acorns, winter wheat, clover, rotting potatoes, rotting fruit and weeds of all sorts. However, local migration takes place in December for the birds to find the easiest source of food available and they usually only move a very few miles to ... yes, you've guessed it, winter oilseed rape.

Difficult to decoy in December, unless the weather is right for the job. Terrific bags when the wind and the barometer are right, but usually few and far between.

Roost shooting now starts in earnest where there are no pheasants. The leaf is off the tree and darkness comes soon after four o'clock. Great sport, but don't count the cartridges!

JANUARY

January tends to be similar to December, but the birds are warier now. The gas guns are well and truly on, along with all the other scaring devices we see: flappers, scarecrows, kites, whirligigs, whistles, sirens and the like. None of them very effective, but they do make the pigeon very twitchy and less and less easy to decoy. Still on rape, their crops are stuffed so full in the late afternoon that they come home to roost hardly able to see where they are going.

One of the more interesting features I have noticed about January pigeon over the years is that this is the month they start to lose weight, down to around a pound or so (450 grams). If they survive January and February, they will live to breed again in the spring. The other interesting point is that in my experience the last berry the pigeon goes for is that of the ivy. Maybe it is more poisonous before January? Anyway, I rarely see crops full of these berries before late January.

FEBRUARY

The traditional month for roost shooting. The pheasant season is over, the keeper has caught up his birds and we are allowed into the big woods at last. I personally shoot on as few keepered estates as possible as I like my roost shooting in December and January as well as February. However, I am more fortunate than some, and also my job in winter mainly consists of walking cold rape fields trying to be a mobile scarecrow, so perhaps I earn my extra months' roost shooting.

Decoying in February is a matter of catch as catch can. There is usually the odd good day on the rape and sometimes very early spring-drilled crops right at the end of the month and in the southern half of the country.

MARCH

Ah, spring drilling at last! First, biology again. The days are getting longer and the flocks split up, making birds easier to decoy. They move in ones and twos or small flights of twenty to fifty birds, not as a huge mass of 1,000 or more. The weather is brighter, that beloved west wind is starting to blow again and the farmer is ready to get his tractors, planters, rollers, etc. out of winter hibernation.

Watch out for peas and beans as they are the favourites, mainly because of spilled seed on the surface and the fact that after three months of green vegetable leaves, they once again provide a source of protein in large lumps. This is the last month of roost shooting for me, as the birds are preparing to pair up and the leaf is coming back to the tree.

APRIL

The birds are pairing up now, the days are getting longer all the time and peas and beans are just beginning to show above the ground, perfect for decoying. Equally good, the spring rape is being planted as well as the spring cereals: wheat, barley and oats. There has also been linseed over the last few years (which seems to be grown mainly for subsidies), which the birds will take over the first few weeks but seem to give a miss once it is more than a few inches high.

Towards the very end of the month, the winter rape will be growing very fast and will soon flower. The pigeon will at last move off the crop until harvest time comes around.

MAY

Spring is well and truly here now and the hedgerows provide a feast of buds (hawthorns are particularly favoured, as are apple buds). There is food everywhere, but the scene is ever-changing. The winter rape acreage is a bright yellow carpet of flower, not many pigeon in there, but the spring rape is still highly decoyable. So are the peas, but the beans will have grown too high by now. The sun is warm and the good days are here. As you can see from the graph, a season of plenty.

JUNE

Winter cereals are forming heads and very often the stems cannot support the weight of the early summer rain and wind and the crops, barley and wheat in particular, are laid flat. The pigeon, ever vigilant for an easy meal, zoom in to the laid patches and lay waste great areas every year. The farmer tears his hair out and gets on the phone to you. Remember, if you shoot over laid corn, that birds are easy to decoy but hard to pick. Alternatively, the peas are still decoyable and the birds much easier to pick. Personally I shoot little in June but, I must add, that is my own choice.

JULY

More laid corn, the wheat usually follows the barley. But what we are really waiting for is harvest, which starts any time from the middle to

Magpie at pigeon nest

the end of the month, first the barley, then the winter rape. Joy, oh joy! Perhaps the biggest draw ever for pigeon is a freshly harvested field of rape. The reason? Well, the seed is so small and slippery that a considerable percentage never makes the barn. It falls in front of the combine and alongside it as it moves through the four to five-foot high rape plants. There is seed everywhere, and it is apparently highly sought after if the numbers I have shot at this time are anything to go by. The pigeons must know from the amount of machinery and activity that there is food to be had in abundance and, better still, just lying on the ground ready to be taken.

AUGUST

The feast continues and next on the list after rape and barley come the peas. This really is bonanza time, with warm, sunny weather, soft breezes and pigeon everywhere. Now is the time you can set up a hide at five o'clock in the afternoon and shoot until seven or half past seven in the evening.

Another bonus, of course, is the fact that the winter rape fields over which you toiled to keep the birds off in January and February have been left alone since the rape grew too high for the pigeon to feed in. Now, immediately after the combine is out of the field, you can go back to the same hide site as you had in winter and have 'first time over' all over again.

Combine

SEPTEMBER

This is the last month of my personal year and there is a gradual tailing off after the bumper days of August. The rape and barley stubbles have been ploughed in by now so that the pigeon has to cope with a reduced acreage from which to glean his nourishment. But the beans, the spring rape and the wheat will now be ready for cutting so there are more days to be enjoyed yet.

Over the last few years, I have taken fewer and fewer pigeon from wheat stubble and the reason seems to be that the combine, so careless with the tiny rape seed, is super-efficient with the grains of wheat, and almost nothing is left on the ground after the harvest is over. Beans, on the other hand, are rather like peas: the machines spill many and the pigeon seem to love them.

	Winter OS rape	Spring OS rape	Peas	Beans	Barley	Wheat	Linseed	Setaside	Clover	Acorns etc.	Berries	Stubbles
October				X	X	X	X	X		X	X	X
November				X		X		X	X	X	X	
December	X			X		X		X	X	X	X	
January	X							X	X		X	
February	X							X	X			
March	X		X	X	X	X		X	X			
April		X	X	X	X	X	X	X	X			
May		X	X				X	X	X			
June		X	X		X			X				
July	X		X		X	X		X				X
August	X		X		X	X		X				X
September	X	X	X	X		X		X			X	X

Year Chart

That then is my complete year. There is always some shooting to be had, no matter what the month, and this is one of the great joys of hunting a quarry all the year round. Both hunter and hunted have to pit their wits against all the varying elements of the different seasons, and the weather that comes with the changes. To keep things tidy, I find it useful to chart the different crops and different months to see what my little grey friends may be eating at any time of the year. But, don't forget, the best guide to where they are is what the shot ones have in their crops.

You will notice from the chart that I have left quite a margin for some planting and harvesting dates to allow for the vagaries of the Great British 'snow in April, floods in August' syndrome. However, you should very easily be able to plan your reconnaissance, perhaps even your whole year's shooting, from this information.

A.B.

4

How

RECONNAISSANCE

Having learnt what we are going to shoot, where and when we are going to shoot it, we now need to look at how we are going to go about shooting it. If there is one word that is more important than any other in the world of pigeon shooting, it is reconnaissance. The Oxford English Dictionary defines reconnaissance as, 'Military or naval examination of land to locate enemy or ascertain strategic features. Preliminary survey made by anyone for any purpose.' In our case the survey relates directly to the finding of pigeons and where to site the hide and decoys so that we can most effectively shoot the birds. My own definition of the word is, 'Looking for flight lines and how and where pigeon enter and exit the field on which I want to shoot.'

All sedentary pigeons, in my opinion, live in their own particular areas, which we could call 'parishes'. These parishes, which I do not see as being more than a few square miles in area, contain woods to roost and breed in, water to drink and enough food to support the pigeon population. The routes by which the pigeon travel around their parish are known as flight lines. There are routes from wood to water, from water to food, from food to wood and many other combinations which will be defined by wind, weather, disturbance by shooters, farm work and many other factors. These flight lines, in the main, remain constant in the parish for as long as there are pigeons there. It is widely believed, for example, that the parents teach the young birds the flight lines around their parish as soon as the squabs are able to fly.

It appears to me that one of the main reasons that decoying works at all is because of flight lines. What happens is something like this. You watch the field and see that pigeon fly across it in a very particular way. For example they cross over the hedge, turn right then head for the lone tree standing in the middle of the field and from there veer a little to the left and leave the field through the gap in the hedge between the two tall ash trees. You have now found a flight line. We know that the woodpigeon is a gregarious creature and likes to spend time with, and eat with, his friends. We also believe that all the pigeon in a particular parish use the same flight lines all their lives. So, you find the flight line, build your hide and put out your decoys under that line and it is a fair assumption that all the pigeon which fly along that particular line that day will fly over, or fairly close to, your decoys. It is also known that when pigeon are disturbed they usually fly off along a known flight line (presumably because familiarity means safety to them).

Let us pretend we are a pigeon for a moment. There we are flying along our normal flight line when we spot, directly below our flight path, what appear to be a dozen or so of our friends feeding away merrily on some peas. We obviously want to drop in to join them, but, as we do, we hear a loud noise (not for the first time that day) and, taking fright, we fly away as fast as we can. And where do we fly? Along a known flight line, of course. The pigeon shooter therefore knows that when the pigeon start flying again after the disturbance caused by his shot, they will nearly always fly along their known lines of flight, and so come back to his decoys.

Furthermore, I think that by shooting under a flight line you start a sort of chain reaction. A bird comes in to your decoys, is shot, and drops dead into the pattern. Another bird, flying along the same flight line, sees the first bird drop, and quite naturally follows him into the pattern so that he may join his friends feeding on the ground. You have now started the chain and other birds further back along the line will be encouraged to join the queue to get into the decoys as quickly as they can!

If there were no flight lines and pigeon flew indiscriminately around the area in which they lived there would be very little decoying at all. The simple fact of being under a flight line means that virtually all the pigeon traffic will pass either directly over you or, if not over, certainly near enough for your decoys to do their work and attract birds within range of your gun. Flight lines are not very wide, generally under twenty-five yards. I have a rule of thumb, which I call 'Batley's fifty-yard rule', which says: 'If you are fifty yards off a flight line you will only get fifty per cent of what you would have got if you were directly under the flight line.'

Reconnaissance is very important. Most pigeon shooters go out on the only day that they have free, spy some pigeons on Farmer X's land, carry all their kit over to where they have seen them feeding and set up their decoys, only to find, more often than not, that the birds fly away after the first few shots, never to return. The successful decoyer, on the other hand, will have been to that particular field two or three times already, and will have studied the movement and feeding habits of the birds which he hopes to shoot.

Why several times? Think about your own behaviour when travelling. Let us assume that you are on your way to work in your car and you hear on your radio that there is a traffic jam ahead. You will generally start looking for an alternative route for the next portion of your journey and then revert to your known route as soon as you have successfully passed the jammed road. Again, if you know there are to be roadworks on your normal route you will work out an alternative route for the time that the roadworks take and then automatically return to the familiar run which you have been using for years. I firmly believe that pigeons travel around their parishes in much the same way. It therefore follows that regular reconnaissance is essential. If you go and look at your field on only one occasion it may well be that you have chosen a 'roadworks' day and that when you return three days later there is not a pigeon to be seen anywhere in the sky. The 'roadworks' are finished and all the pigeon have reverted to their normal flight line. ('Roadworks', in pigeon terms, can mean anything from a change in the wind or disturbance by farm machinery, to the felling of a wood on a nearby farm.)

What is more, it appears that pigeon, being inquisitive birds, will drop in to have a look if they see something inviting well away from the line. Another pigeon, happily flying along the flight line, will see his friend alight on the ground and veer off the line to join him. Before you know where you are there are a hundred pigeon, all way off the normal flight line, feasting on whatever is going. Along comes our pigeon shooter and, without a thought about where these birds have come from, sets up shop only to see the birds fly away, never to return. They have gone back to the routes they know and feel safe on, and our pigeon shooter has got nothing for all his efforts. Would it not be better to go and watch the field for a few hours over a period of several days and *then* set up shop directly under the flight line which you have discovered? If there is one vital axiom in reconnaissance, it is surely, 'Look for birds in the air not on the ground.' 'Look for pigeon traffic,' as Archie Coats so often used to say.

So how do we go about finding flight lines and deciding where to build our hides and set up our decoys? First of all we need binoculars. As finding pigeons and their lines of flight is of paramount importance to me as I earn my living from it, I have never stinted when it comes to binoculars. I have two pairs, one for use from the vehicle, and a second which is extremely lightweight and which I can easily carry in my pocket.

The larger pair are 10×42, quite adequate for all my pigeon shooting needs, and I think that $\times 10$ magnification is about as high as one can easily hand hold. Anything greater than 10s really needs a tripod as one cannot hold them steady enough to get a clear picture. The field of view, at 42, is quite wide enough for the level of light in which I use the binoculars. The second pair I use mainly from the hide, and they live almost permanently in my waistcoat pocket. They are 7×20 and are very useful for checking out details in the more immediate vicinity. Neither pair was cheap, costing well over £100 each, but I think they are well worth the money. If I were asked to recommend a pair of binoculars for the amateur pigeon shooter I would suggest a robust pair of 8×30s costing around £50.

Right, we've got some binoculars, let's go and find some pigeons. There are two ways of going about this. One, to be phoned by a friendly farmer, or two, to go out into virgin territory and find the birds for ourselves. In the first case, you may well arrive at the farm to be told that there are pigeon feeding on the field of beans down by the stream. You drive as close as possible to the field, and, sure enough, there they are, 300 birds busily tucking into the freshly drilled field which all fly away as you approach. You sit quietly and twenty minutes later they start to return. At this point you still have no idea of how they get in or out of the field – they just seem to appear as if by magic.

Pigeons, where possible, like to fly *along* the contours, not over them, so the first thing that you must do is to look for any slopes or undulating ground in the field in which your quarry is feeding. The next thing is wind direction. Woodpigeon are happiest flying into the wind (it is easier using the wind to lift you, as does an aeroplane, than having it blowing into your tail and making you unstable). Compass points and directions are important to pigeon shooters. The prevailing wind in this country comes from the south-west so you should expect your pigeons to fly from east to west across the field. But how do you work out the wind direction (in order to site a hide) during reconnaissance on new ground on a windless, cloudy day?

There are a number of tricks, starting with basics like the sun rising in the east, passing through south at roughly midday and setting in the west. There are other points as well. All Anglican churches used to be built with the nave running east – west, the altar facing east. Most houses (especially old ones) in the country were built facing south (for maximum use of sunlight for light and heat, before electricity and central heating). Moss grows on the northern side of a tree. Most barns with one open side have the open side towards the east (since the rain in Great Britain comes mainly from the west). Most rivers flow either east or west towards the sea.

The next point is that pigeon are afraid of birds of prey, especially sparrow hawks, and sparrow hawks fly up and down hedgerows looking for quarry so, it would make enormous sense for a pigeon to cross over a hedge by flying through a gap in the hedge through which it can see the other side before it crosses.

Now you are beginning to build a picture of what to look for in your search for a flight line. It gets better and easier. Pigeons like to stop off from time to time on their journey around their parish, so perhaps the next thing to look for is a staging post, or 'sitty tree' as Archie Coats used to call them. Are there any highish single trees in your field, perhaps an ash in the hedgerow or if you are lucky an old oak in the middle of the field? Next, how about water? Is there any stream, river or pond anywhere near your field? If there is, there is a strong chance that your birds will visit it from time to time to drink. Then, is there a line of pylons, or power wires running across your field which is clearly visible from the air? If so, there is a strong chance that pigeon will use it as part of their flight line.

So, what was just a field at first glance has become somewhere that contains all sorts of features which pigeon might use in going about their daily business in their parish. All you have to do now is settle down with your binoculars and watch how the birds enter and leave the field and decide where best to site your hide .

What I try to do when I first look at a field which I hope to shoot is metaphorically take my eyes out, and put them fifty feet up in the air. I try and look at the field below as a pigeon would. A lot of features which we see from six feet or so above the ground look completely different from fifty feet up. For instance, a row of pylons will always be in the open and will act almost as a road. It will be very easy to follow from the air whereas on the ground you may only be able to see two or three at any one time. On my own patch, I have a line of pylons which I reckon stretch more than four miles from east to west and there are approximately ten places almost under these lines where I have successfully decoyed pigeon.

To summarise, here are a list of the major features which go to make up a flight line and which we need to consider when we are doing reconnaissance:

1. Hills and slopes. Pigeons will fly along rather than over contours.
2. Wind direction. Pigeons will more often fly into the wind than with it behind them. The prevailing wind in Great Britain is from the southwest.
3. Sitty trees. Look for single high trees, which are used as staging posts.
4. Hedges. These help in navigation and provide protection from the wind (by using the lee side).
5. Gaps in hedges. Pigeons prefer to fly through rather than over gaps, because of the danger from birds of prey.
6. Pylon lines. These are probably used as navigational aids ('roads').
7. Rivers and streams. Pigeons need to drink, and rivers and streams also act as navigational aids like pylon lines.
8. Farm Buildings. Pigeons will try and avoid buildings and disturbance by people and machinery.
9. Minor roads and tracks. These are almost certainly used as navigational aids.

Remember to try to look at the countryside as if from the air and always try and think above the field rather than on it. You can now see that even when you are going into virgin territory, the task is much easier than it first appears. All you have to do is go and look at a farm where you have permission to shoot and even if there are no birds immediately apparent, you can see where they should be by following the guidelines above.

What you need to do is sit with the binoculars and watch where you reckon the pigeons *should* fly, and once you have spotted a few which seem to travel across the field using the same route, you will almost

Flight line

certainly have found their flight line. It takes no more than a dozen or so birds to establish the line and perhaps an hour or so to confirm that there are birds moving on that particular line on that particular day.

The need for reconnaissance on more than one day is paramount; remember the 'roadworks' syndrome. Before I shoot a field, I hope to have watched the flight line for at least three hours spread over as many days. If possible, I will go early in the morning of the first day, at midday on the second and in the afternoon of the third. This will generally give me a pretty complete picture of the pigeon activity on that field and it will also tell me what is the best time of the day to shoot it. You will not have failed to notice that at no time have I recommended going to the field and merely looking at any birds that may be feeding on the ground. What I am primarily interested in is where the birds are flying and how to get my hide directly under the flight line.

There are any number of anecdotes about reconnaissance, but the one that I like the best goes as follows. A pigeon shooter rang me up in a fine old temper. The reason? I had a pea field of some twenty-two acres on which I had shot around 700 birds from planting to harvest, and the flight line over this field was so classic that I wrote an article about it for my 'Pigeon Forum' column in *Shooting Times*. In particular, the line was so strongly defined that if I moved fifty yards from it, I hardly got any birds in to the decoys at all. There really was only one place to be. Anyway, my caller was having none of this. I was a liar, there was no way anyone could shoot 700 pigeons on a twenty-two acre field of peas.

The reason, it transpired, was that the gentleman in question also had a twenty-two acre field of peas and he had shot only twenty pigeons! Apparently there were always pigeon all over his field and he could not get them to come to his decoys, however hard he tried. After a great deal of questioning we managed to work out why. Right at the start of the proceedings, when the peas had been planted, our pigeon shooter had been told by the farmer that the field was 'blue' with pigeons and, sure enough, when he went to have a look there were plenty on the ground scavenging all the loose peas left on the surface during planting. In particular they were sitting conveniently near to a clump of elder bushes which bordered the field. So, without further ado the chap set up a hide in the bushes and had been visiting the spot every week or so from April to late August. Total bag in all this time? Just over twenty. 'Were there always pigeons flying over the field?' I asked. 'Yes, always!' 'And where exactly were these pigeons?' 'Oh, 250 yards further down the hedgerow,

Sparrowhawk hunting woodpigeon

flying backwards and forwards all day long!' This is a perfect example of going to where the pigeons are feeding and not where they are flying.

In the last ten years I can only recall one spectacular day on which I carried out no reconnaissance at all and got away with it. Normally if I just turn up and set up my hide and decoys where the birds are feeding I get what I deserve for doing no prior reconnaissance and have to move everything to get under the flight line.

HIDES AND HIDE BUILDING

Having done our reconnaissance and looked at the field which we want to shoot, we are convinced that the flight line crosses over the hedge about 150 yards down from the gateway. The next thing we need to do is build a hide and get on with decoying pigeons. On the face of it, building a hide seems to be a very simple procedure: a gap in a hedge, a few branches strategically placed, add some foliage, put the kit and dog inside and you are set for the day. However, nature and Murphy's Law have a way of intervening. There always seems to be a marked lack of spare branches of the right size and length lying about for you to use and you know full well that the farmer, on whom you rely for all your shooting, will be hopping mad if you cut any of his hawthorn or other

Construction of Natural Hide

precious trees. So just as reconnaissance has to be done properly and methodically, so does hide building.

We are probably all familiar with the art of camouflage from tales of soldiers and war on television, but it is wise to remember that our 'enemy' is a bird, not another human being, and our needs and approach to camouflage therefore differ from those of the soldier. Personally I do not believe that it is absolutely necessary to conceal the hide from the bird. That is not to say that I advocate sticking it right in the middle of a bare field, but it does mean that you can quite happily set your hide on the outside of a hedge or at the base of a tree without worrying too much about the consequences. The crucial thing, to my mind, is that there should be no movement visible to the incoming bird. Providing that your hide blends fairly well with its surroundings and you are able to see the approaching bird without moving, you stand a good chance of getting a bag.

For all types of hide there are a few golden rules. The first is probably that our hides are intended to distort the vision of the 'enemy', rather than hide us completely from him. The second is that when we build a hide of any type we must remember that there are no straight lines in nature and try to build our hides accordingly. The third is that we must build a hide that enables us to sit, or stand, in comfort and be able to see what our quarry is doing without moving. I would add a fourth which says that today's hide should be light and portable, and if you are using camouflage netting it should be lighter rather than darker in colour.

There are basically three types of pigeon hide: natural, bale and nets. Let us look at the advantages, and disadvantages, of each type and see which best suits our needs.

The natural hide is exactly what it says. It is made of natural material taken from the pigeon shooter's immediate surroundings on the day on which he is shooting. It has the enormous advantage of blending in without the addition of any artificial material and can be abandoned after it is finished with. For example, on a farm which grows fruit or potatoes there are quite often pallets or large wooden boxes to be found which can make superb hides. The pigeon are quite used to seeing these pallets and boxes and are not at all frightened by their presence. Agricultural machinery, either abandoned or merely parked, can form the basis of a natural hide, and the simple addition of a camouflage net can make you almost invisible within a matter of minutes. In my youth we used to use three sheep hurdles and a piece of tank netting very successfully.

By far the most common form of natural hide is one that is built either in a hedge or on the edge of a wood, and we should look at the pros and cons of such a hide as well as how to build one. In favour of such a hide are the facts that it is easy to build, there is nothing to carry on to or off the field, it blends with its surroundings, there are no poles or nets to buy and the shape and size can be changed at will. Unfortunately, it is difficult to get the gaps to see through without moving all the time. It is also likely to have branches and the like which get in the way when you are swinging the gun, it can be awkward to get the dog in or out without damaging the structure of the hide, and it is sometimes very hard to find the materials that you need without having to cut precious timber. Worst of all, the obvious temptation is to go to where it is easiest to build a hide rather than under the flight line. So on balance, I am not very keen on natural hides, although I am the first to admit that they do have their place and I have had some great days shooting from them.

In order to build a natural hide, you will need a dozen or so branches stout enough to carry the weight of the foliage that you will use to dress it and straight enough to be rammed into the ground as the main uprights. Ideally the hide should be at least three feet square to give you room enough to sit, stand and shoot and your dog enough space to sit or lie in comfort when he is not working.

Basically what you should aim for is a structure that resembles that of a five-bar gate or sheep hurdle in front of you over which you may drape or entwine natural foliage, and another lighter hurdle, also draped in foliage, over the top of you to act as a roof. Of course this is the ideal, and most of us seem to do only half the job because there are not enough branches available and we end up being seen by the incoming pigeon which promptly jinks away from the decoys before it is really in range.

If you are determined that natural is best, I can pass on a few tips I have learned over the years which may be of some help. Firstly, never use baler twine to tie up your branches or stakes. 'Bungees' are the modern equivalent and require no tying or cutting. Secondly, there is no need to carry a heavy bill-hook for cutting branches; a modern folding pruning saw only weighs a few ounces and is perhaps even more effective than the bill-hook. Thirdly, always make a good entrance and exit to your hide so that you and the dog are not scrambling either over or under the hide in your attempts to get in or out. Fourthly, always take down the structure after you have finished shooting, otherwise you will have someone else coming along and taking advantage of your hide when you are not there. This last point is not just a petty gesture. Pigeons are not stupid and if they are constantly being shot at from one place they will bend their flight line to avoid that place.

Whenever I am tempted to use natural cover as the basis for a hide I always ask myself two questions. Firstly, is the natural cover really under the flight line? And secondly, am I just being lazy in trying to avoid carrying a net and poles all the way across the field? I am afraid to tell you that the answer to the first question is usually no, and to the second, yes! There seems little point in having taken the time and trouble to do your reconnaissance if you waste the opportunity for some shooting by having a hide either in the wrong place or one that is not up to scratch.

The second type of hide that is sometimes available to us is the bale hide. Like other types, these hides have both advantages and disadvantages, and it is as well to look at these before you start lugging bales around a field. The advantages are simple. Firstly, a bale hide is the only one that you can site in the middle of a field without the pigeons immediately becoming suspicious and bending their line of flight away from the hide. Secondly, by being able to site your hide in the middle of the field you give the birds more room to swing in to your decoys. Thirdly, no matter where the wind is coming from you can always shoot with it at your back, offering you the easiest shot in the book. Fourthly, bales are fairly dense and offer you more protection from the cold on a bleak winter's day.

Hide made from round bales

You would think that all these advantages would automatically outweigh any disadvantages, but unfortunately that is not so. Thirty years ago bale hides were *the* thing – indeed both Archie Coats and John Ransford took their world record bags from them. But nowadays things have changed. Farmers seem to need less and less straw and very often sell it 'standing', so that a contractor comes on to the farm and bales and removes it as soon as it is combined, leaving you little or no chance to use a bale hide at harvest time. Furthermore, if there is no straw left on the farm you have no raw material for your bale hide during the winter months on the rape. But if you do get the chance, there is no doubt in my mind that shooting from a bale hide in the middle of a field is one of the best pigeon shooting experiences available. The spectacle of a pigeon on a windless day in summer turning in his flight across a field and, at 200 feet above the ground, closing his wings and swooping down to the decoys set around a bale hide is one which I hold very dear and one which I sadly see less and less of these days.

To build a bale hide using the traditional small rectangular bales, you need about sixteen of them to be comfortable. You simply treat them like outsize house bricks and construct them into a small house with enough room inside for you, the dog and the kit. Have the back of the hide higher than the front so that you have background cover, and use one of the bales as a seat. Leave a small gap on one of the sides as a way in and out for you and the dog, and a good idea in these days of warier pigeons is to put a small net over the top as a roof. Sadly the small rectangular bale seems to have acquired a bigger brother which weighs more than I can carry single-handedly, so, if you see a field full of these 'big brothers' and want to shoot it, remember to take a friend along with you.

Nowadays the round bale appears to be the norm at harvest time. Luckily for us they are extremely easy to turn into pigeon hides and are relatively easy to move into place under a flight line. You only need three of these bales plus a small net to make a very adequate hide. All you have to do is to roll them together to form an open fronted 'U' and then drape a net across the front. Let me give you a word of advice on how to roll the bales on the field. Bend your knees, put both hands against the bale and then straighten up from the crouching position and you will find that it will roll quite easily, and once mobile it is quite easy to keep moving. If you try and push the bale from the top you will find that you do not have the necessary leverage to get the operation started. But be warned: several hundredweight of round bale on the move, even down a slight slope, is virtually unstoppable, so please be careful. A couple of years ago a small child was severely injured by a runaway round bale.

There have been many changes in farming since I started shooting, and perhaps the most obvious of these is the reduction in the labour force. This is never more evident than when you need to ask the farmer a favour which is going to cost him money in terms of labour. It is a costly business to take a man off some other work in order to take a tractor and trailer loaded with bales across a field in late autumn so that a pigeon shooter can have some 'fun' in winter. It is even more costly to take two men off a job in spring, just before you need to spray the field of rape, to take a tractor and trailer back to collect sixteen very heavy wet bales off that same field. Try to offer your farmer some compensation for all the extra work you have caused him. I know that you were only there to help protect his rape crop, but he will never remember that unless the pigeons were actually hammering the field on the very day that the bales were set up or removed!

So there you have it, some of the advantages and disadvantages of both natural and bale hides. I have to say that my own preference for the 1990s is a net hide. One thing that stands out in all the literature on pigeon shooting is the change in the quarry over the years. I think therefore that as pigeon shooters we must be aware of these changes and keep up to date with them by refining our methods of hunting our quarry.

One of the most important changes is in the pigeons' habits of small commando raids to feeding places and their ability to move from place to place as their needs dictate. To keep up with the birds, we have to be more flexible and be prepared to move our hides at a moment's notice. There is nothing worse than building a hide in a hedgerow and then realising after perhaps an hour or so that it is in the wrong place, and that to get a bag you need to move perhaps several hundred yards to get under the line. This is where a net hide comes into its own.

Twenty years ago a net hide meant steel poles weighing several pounds each plus an ex-army camouflage net which weighed some ten pounds dry and twice as much when wet. Even then it was always portable and offered one the opportunity of moving at short notice without too much difficulty, but nowadays a net hide need not weigh more that ten pounds at the absolute maximum, and can often weigh as little as six or seven. My own hide weighs just over eight pounds and includes five poles, twenty feet of netting, a roof net and the carrying bag.

A net hide was traditionally constructed with four poles and a separate net or nets. The poles were pushed into the ground in the form of a square and, using the hedgerow as background, the net was draped around the poles making a very effective hide. This is how I, and many others, made our hides for years. When I started commercial pigeon shooting and was looking after guests, who were perhaps less experienced than I was, I would build the hide, install the guest and retire to my vehicle to watch the proceedings with binoculars. I would very often be a quarter of a mile or more away from the hide and in a perfect position to see how both the guest and the pigeons performed. From that distance it very quickly became obvious that what I thought was a good hide was not very good at all.

Firstly, whenever the Gun stood up or moved a little too fast, the movements could be seen from a long way off. So although the pigeon in the decoys would often be shot, the second and third ones which were approaching along the flight line would jink away while the Gun was concentrating on the one which he was shooting. Equally, any pigeon approaching from above and behind would easily see him and turn off before getting anywhere near the pattern. Secondly, I was very limited in my choice of hide site because of the need for background cover. And thirdly, the Gun would very often catch his gun in the net in front of him as he rose to take a shot or broke the gun to reload.

So I did a lot of thinking about camouflage and hides in general, and I gradually developed the net hide which I now use, in one form or another, at all times and for all people. The hide needed to be portable,

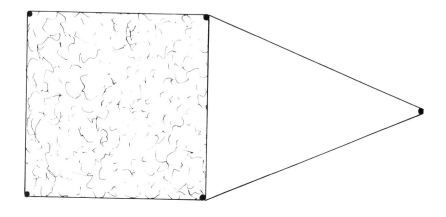

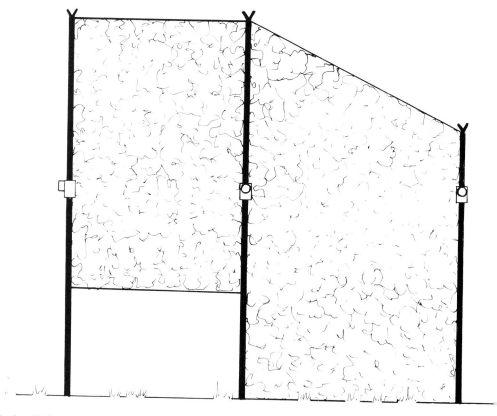

The John Batley Hide

have its own background, be variable in height, be fast to erect and take down, and allow an inexperienced Gun to use it without being spotted by the pigeons, whether from in front, behind or above. It also needed to have a good 'door' to let the less athletic in and out and the front net needed to be placed so that guns would not constantly be getting entangled. Moreover, it had to be able to be placed under a tree right in the middle of a field without the occupant being spotted by the pigeons. Quite a tall order! But after many false starts and many modifications I think that I have cracked it.

You will see from the diagrams that my hides bear little resemblance to the old-fashioned four-pole structure, but they do meet all the criteria needed to make my clients happy and almost invisible to the incoming pigeons. The five poles are made of aluminium and are adjustable from three feet six inches to almost seven feet. The net is twenty feet by five feet and permanently attached to four of the poles so that the hide is always the same size and shape. The 'background' is integral to the structure, thus making the choice of hide site much easier. The roof net is kept separately and can be used quite easily on its own when roost shooting. The fifth pole is used to make the front of the hide into an inverted 'V' so that the incoming pigeon has its vision distorted by the acute angle of the net. (The Gun on the inside has the corresponding wide angle to look out of.) The 'V' has the further advantage of making it nearly impossible to foul the gun in the net when loading or unloading. The front 'V' drapes on the ground whilst the two sides are left eighteen inches or so above the ground so that the dog can get in and out easily. With the front net looped over the top of the first pole, there is a perfectly good 'door' for easy access. (No more scrabbling around in the hedge on your hands and knees trying to get in or out.)

With a four-pole hide you will have great difficulty erecting it under a tree, as the roots always seem to impede the two poles nearest the tree, making the hide stand out too far from the tree for easy concealment. But erect my hide at the base of a tree is simplicity itself. Push the two front poles into the ground roughly three feet in front of the tree and extend them up to about five feet. Extend the two back poles to about the same height and lean them against the tree about three feet apart. Take one or two 'bungees' and stretch them around the back of the tree from one pole to the other, thus fixing the two rear poles in position against the tree. Now raise all four poles to your optimum height, put in the fifth pole to make your 'V', pop on the roof and you are ready to put out the decoys and start shooting.

The idea for the 'V' at the front of the hide came about by one of those strange, and lucky, coincidences which happen to us all from time to

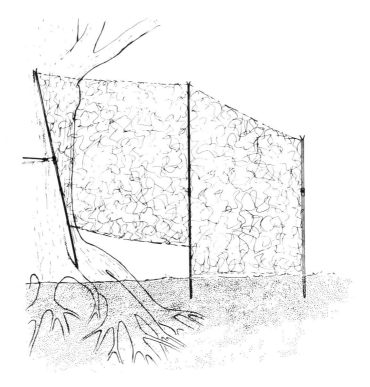

time. I had a Frenchman shooting with me one summer who, although an excellent shot, was forever getting his gun caught up in the net every time he reloaded. At that time I was halfway through the development of the hide, and was still using a square structure. After two days, during which I was constantly going from Land Rover to hide and back again in order to keep rebuilding the front of the hide, I suddenly hit on an idea – stick an extra pole in front of the hide, drape the front net around it in the form of a 'V' and the Gun would never be able to get his gun caught again. I armed myself with an extra pole and marched across the field to the hide; the poor client must have thought that I had violence on my mind! Anyway, I duly stuck the pole in the ground, rearranged the net and marched off again muttering to myself. Halfway back to the vehicle I turned round to admire my handiwork and, lo and behold, I could no longer see the hide properly at all! Quite by accident I had changed all the angles of view and neatly distorted the vision of anything that approached the hide from the front. From that point on every time I think of any changes to the hide I always try and remember to inspect the changes from the pigeon's point of view. Many of the great truisms in pigeon shooting come from the Master himself, Archie Coats, and one of the greatest is: 'Think like a pigeon.' In the case of hides this

means looking at your structure from where the bird itself would see it as it comes into the decoy pattern.

A word or two about the type and colour of the camouflage netting which I use in my hides. Modern military camouflage netting is made from nylon scrim and comes in a variety of colours. I use one that is known as 'Grass Screen', which is considerably lighter in colour than the traditional tank net. I have come to the conclusion over the years that the dark net, which I used to use, is fine in the military sense where it was used in the horizontal plane to disguise tanks and the like from being spotted by aeroplanes. But used in the vertical plane it is so dark that it sticks out on a hedgerow and attracts the eye to it rather than away from it. Moreover, the lighter colour of the 'Grass Screen' seems to be equally as effective against any type of background that you can encounter. I have used it on the edge of conifer plantations in Scotland and against barbed-wire fences in sheep country and found it equally good. Remember that in the context of pigeon shooting, camouflage is intended to distort rather than conceal.

The camouflage scrim should be attached to a net of about three-inch mesh and should offer 100 per cent cover. Once you have tried out the hide a few times, mark it with a felt pen where you need spy holes and cut the scrim (not the net), with a sharp pair of scissors. These spy holes will increase your visibility and enable you to sit still until the pigeon is actually over the decoys before you get up to shoot it. Do not forget to cut one or two holes in the sides of the hide as well as in the front.

To sum up: hides need to distort the vision of the bird not the shooter; they need to be built under the flight line; they should house the shooter, his dog, and his equipment in comfort. If a net hide is used it needs to be light enough to be carried anywhere, and if camouflage netting is utilised it should be light coloured rather than dark.

DECOYS AND DECOYING

I make no apology for not discussing the essence of pigeon shooting (decoying) until this stage in the book. Until one has mastered reconnaissance and hide building, there is no point in approaching the art of decoying.

The shooting of woodpigeon over decoys has been going on for at least a century now and, like everything else in pigeon shooting, has changed radically over the years. At the beginning of the century it was quite legal to use live decoys and the professional market gunners shot huge bags of birds to satisfy the needs of the consumer. Over the last fifty years or so attitudes and the law have both changed and the use of live decoys has been banned in this country; nowadays pigeon are shot over decoys, made of various materials, or dead birds.

Pigeon decoying, either for sport or crop protection, has become a new art and one which is as difficult as it is challenging to master. The results depend mainly on the decoyer's knowledge of fieldcraft and, of course, his ability to shoot straight. When I first took up pigeon shooting in the 1950s I was taught that to be a good pigeon decoyer I first needed to go out and study a flock of feeding pigeons. Once I had done this then I was to try and duplicate the feeding flock with the decoys. You may say that this was an intelligent approach, and at that time I would have agreed with you, but nowadays pigeon have become much more wary; not only do they jink away from a shiny plastic decoy, they actually seem to shy away from a badly laid out pattern.

Over the years I have looked at the basic premise behind using decoys to duplicate a feeding flock and I have come to the conclusion that a new strategy is required. The reasons are quite straightforward. A feeding flock of pigeons is obviously alive and constantly on the move with birds joining it and flying away all the time. Decoys, on the other hand, are static. A feeding flock of pigeons will immediately fly away when a shot is fired at them; decoys will not. What I really need to know is what makes pigeon come to a pattern of decoys rather than what makes it come to a feeding flock of live birds. The first clues came from Archie Coats' use of a 'killing ground'. This looked quite unlike a feeding flock, but it undoubtedly worked. This and other hints made me begin to define what the bird was looking for in a decoy pattern. The results of my thinking are threefold and these are now my main criteria when laying out a pattern:

1. Safety. The pattern must offer a safe place to feed. Pigeon, as we have seen, are prey and I think that if the pattern offers protection on the ground from an attack by a hawk whilst feeding then the pigeon is more likely to come into it.

2. Space. The pattern must be easy to approach and get into. We saw in Chapter One that the pigeon's eyesight only allows for twenty-four degrees of binocular vision and therefore if we can construct an uncluttered pattern which helps it switch to binocular vision, at an early stage in its approach, then we stand a good chance of getting it to fly in to the decoys.

3. Salvation. The pattern must allow sufficient room between the decoys for the bird to make an emergency exit if, in the event of an attack by a predator, it has to overfly the decoys. Remember that the pigeon thinks the decoys are live birds and they have to be overtaken in order to evade the attacker.

So what is needed is protection on the ground whilst feeding, room to get in and room to get out. If you allow for all of these features in your patterns you stand a good chance of successfully decoying today's wary woodpigeon. You should be able to have pigeon landing among your decoys about twenty-five yards away from your hide. Furthermore, if you keep absolutely still and do not attempt to shoot when the birds land, they should stay in the pattern for anything up to half a minute before becoming suspicious and flying away again. On a day when the birds are decoyable, I would go as far as to say that if they do not, when left alone, land in the pattern, then there is something wrong with either your pattern or your hide.

My ten-year-old son James has recently started shooting with his own single-barrelled .410, and to help him with his first flying shots I set up a pattern which had the birds landing ten yards away from us in the hide. I am delighted to report that this did the trick very nicely and James was able to shoot his first two flying pigeon at just under fifteen yards.

All the new patterns I use are tried out by the simple expedient of building a hide, putting out decoys and seeing just how the birds react to each individual situation. On these trial days the gun is left at home – the temptation to use it would be too great! The idea is straightforward: lay out some decoys, allow some pigeons to come and land in the pattern and, when they do, clap them off. I repeat this process several times until I am sure that the pattern is working.

The next step is vital. I change the pattern until I get to a point where the pigeon approach it to within forty yards or so and then jink away. Then I know what it is about the pattern that they don't like, and I should be able to avoid that set-up in the future.

Whenever you lay out a pattern of decoys it is well worth while taking the time to do it properly. Most of us make a hide, stroll out twenty-five yards or so into the field and put out some decoys, then return to the hide, load the gun and sit and wait hopefully for the pigeon to oblige by flying into the decoys. What I think you should do is build the hide, prepare it for shooting by removing the gun from the slip and leaving it unloaded but ready for use, install the dog, tidy up all the spare gear, put a few cartridges in your pocket, then walk out on to the field and lay out the decoys, walk back to the prepared hide and immediately load the gun. Very often the moment we have returned to the hide after putting out the decoys and concealed ourselves a pigeon will appear from nowhere and catch us napping with an unloaded gun.

The reason is fairly obvious. We are on this particular field because there are pigeons there. The moment we arrive to build a hide they fly away, but, we are too busy building a hide and putting out decoys to see how far they fly when we put them up. Usually they do not go very far – after all, they are quite used to seeing people on farms every day of their lives, and furthermore they do not know what we have in mind for them! Pigeons are inquisitive birds, so when they fly off they very often retire to nearby trees and watch the proceedings. The moment that the decoys are in place and the shooter has 'disappeared' by going into his hide, the birds may well do what they are supposed to do and fly down to join their 'friends' on the ground and start feeding.

As I have already said many times, we must look at things from a pigeon's point of view, and this applies equally to laying out decoys. More often than not, we stroll out into the field, put out the decoys and stroll back to the hide. How often do we walk 100 yards or more into the field and look at the decoys as the incoming pigeon will? Not very often I'll wager! We naturally tend to look at things only from man's point of view.

Another important point: never run! Pigeons see people every day. In particular they see farm workers who, in my experience, very rarely run! Everything you do when you are in the field should be calculated to be as natural as possible so as to avoid frightening your quarry. On an average day it will take up to twenty minutes for wildlife to start moving again after you have built your hide and set out your decoys. Pigeon shooting is hunting, so think like a hunter.

Remember, too, that pigeons do not know they are being shot at. This may seem unlikely, but consider all the factors. A dead bird does not go and tell his friends that he has been shot. A wounded bird has no way, to my knowledge, of knowing what caused the wound. A bird that is missed has no idea of anything but the bang that frightened him and caused him to fly away. Pigeons, in my opinion, are fairly short on intelligence but very long on instinct. This instinct makes them fly along flight lines, as their parents did, and it makes them want to come to feeding 'friends' on the ground. Every time there is a bang where do the pigeons go? Back on the flight line.

On the siting of patterns, my view is that one should avoid the edges of woods. The nearer you are to a wood the more places you are giving your pigeons to hide. The nearer you are to the middle of a field the more your pigeons have to fly in the open, therefore the more chance they have of being spotted by other pigeons, thus creating traffic in the air. The more that they can hide in a wood, the less traffic there is in the open air for other birds to see and therefore the fewer chances you have of starting a chain reaction of one pigeon following another into your decoys.

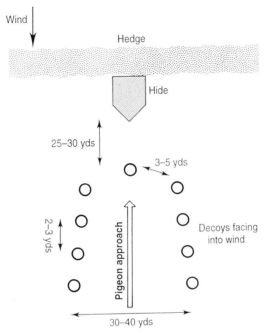

'U' shaped pattern 'horseshoe'.

What we need to do now is look at how many decoys we need to construct a pattern which will meet the three criteria of Safety, Space and Salvation listed on page 71 and then lay them out in a way that pigeon cannot resist.

The diagram shows a traditional 'U' or horseshoe pattern; the hide is in the hedge, and the wind is coming from behind the shooter. The decoy pattern starts about twenty-five yards away from the hide and the decoys are placed three to five yards apart. The open end of the 'U' is around forty yards from the hide and about thirty yards wide. The decoys are placed in fairly regimented lines so as to make the whole pattern as uncluttered as possible. At the front of the pattern the decoys are given wider spacing than in the 'arms'. A maximum of nine decoys is needed for this layout, and I would very seldom use more than this number to start off a pattern. The pigeon approaching this pattern has a wide entrance (Space), plenty of possibilities to overfly the decoys if he needs to get out in a hurry (Salvation), and because of the 'U' shape he can land at the front end of the pattern, taking advantage of the protection offered by the other birds virtually all around him, whilst he is on the ground (Safety).

Pigeons always approach a landing, be it onto a branch or the ground, head into wind and hawks nearly always attack flying head into wind.

In the case of the 'U'-shaped pattern the deeper into the pattern our pigeon flies before landing the safer he will be. An attacking hawk, also approaching head into wind, would take one of the 'birds' on the arms of the pattern thus leaving our recently arrived bird safe from capture. One of the golden rules of this and virtually all other decoy patterns is to keep the inside of the pattern clear at all times, thus allowing the pigeon plenty of space to fly deep into it for safety.

Before I used this system of decoying there were many occasions on which birds would approach the pattern and when they got to about fifty yards away jink away without an apparent reason. I am now firmly of the opinion that my previous patterns were too cluttered for the pigeon to find his way in.

We have seen that the woodpigeon's vision is quite extraordinary, with 340 degrees of monocular vision but only twenty-four degrees of binocular vision. I have already said that it is my belief that he only uses this binocular vision for landing, either on a branch or on the ground, and when he does so he is virtually blind on the sides. It follows that if you are trying to land in a cluttered area you will be very vulnerable to attack from a predator if you are constantly switching your vision from monocular to binocular and back again. Far better to have things laid out like an airport runway where you can see from afar exactly where to land and switch your vision from the vigilant flying mode to the landing mode at the last moment. Of course, all this is, of necessity, speculation. I don't know for sure exactly what the pigeon sees as he comes in to land in the decoys. What I do know, however, is that the system works. Over the years my bags have been consistently better than they were when I was using the 'duplicate the feeding flock' method.

There are three other basic decoy patterns which I use, although all of them have many minor variations depending on the wind direction first and foremost, and of course on the amount of space available. As we can see from the diagrams, all of these patterns are laid out using clearly defined lines that are fairly regimented in their construction and nearly all the decoys are positioned with their heads into wind. One of my most favourite patterns is the 'L' shape. When it works well the pigeon come into it as if on rails. On a really good day when the wind is blowing at least force four at right angles to the hide, the birds seem to come in to the pattern as if they were all equipped with tape measures, to make sure that they fly down the exact middle of the long side of the 'L' before trying to land just before reaching the short side of the pattern.

I once had two Guns out shooting who, although extremely experienced in other forms of shooting, had never shot pigeon over decoys

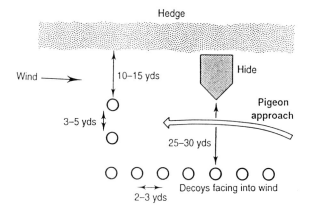

'L' shaped pattern. Wind from right.

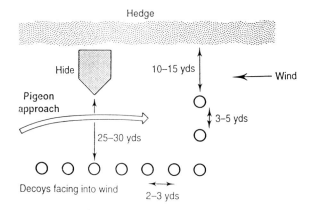

'L' shaped pattern. Wind from left.

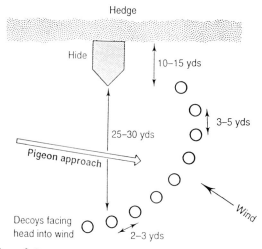

'Curve pattern. Wind from left.

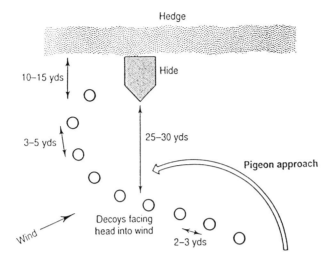

'Curve' pattern. Wind from right.

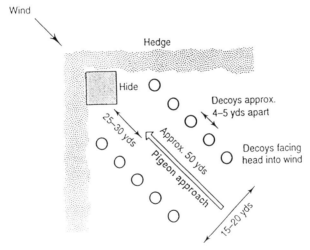

Parallel lines. For use in corner of field. Wind from behind.

before. The wind was blowing hard and the pigeon came into my 'L'-shaped pattern as if radio controlled, one after the other, in ones and twos for almost two hours – one of those very rare occasions when you forget that the bird is wild. The Guns must have shot almost sixty, and I was sitting at the back of the hide, as happy as Larry, when the blow struck. 'Mr Batley,' said one of the Guns, 'can we go and stand in that wood over there please?'

'Why?' I asked innocently, still with my large grin intact from the sheer pleasure of seeing the birds behave as if drilled by a sergeant major.

'Because, Mr Batley, this is boring. You set up the decoys, birds come in one after the other, on exactly the same line into exactly the same place and there is no challenge to the shooting. We think standing in the wood would present more of a challenge!' There was no reply. I was sitting at the back of the hide, gently weeping.

There are common factors in all decoying situations.

1. Distance from the hide to first decoys. Twenty-five to thirty yards is the norm. This has little to do with the pigeon but a lot to do with the shooter and his gun. Most guns pattern best at between twenty-five and thirty-five yards so it makes sense to have your decoys and killing ground placed at that distance.

2. Killing ground. This is an expression first used by Archie Coats many years ago to describe the empty space which he left at the front of his decoy pattern where he wanted to kill his birds. The concept is, in my opinion, still very relevant to today's decoying methods and I always leave that area as empty as I can.

3. Numbers of decoys. I am firmly convinced that, initially, it is not the quantity of decoys which attracts the birds to the pattern but rather the way in which they are laid out. Somewhere between eight and a dozen decoys to start with should cover virtually every situation.

4. Space between decoys. Allow three to five yards between each decoy; again remember shape of pattern rather than density.

5: Addition of shot birds to the pattern. As a general rule of thumb birds should be added to the pattern as they are picked. The first ones should replace any artificial decoys in your pattern and anything else should be used to build up the original picture.

6. Artificial or dead birds. I am convinced that dead birds always work better.
   (If you have no dead birds try and make sure that your artificial decoys do not shine too much in the sun or the rain.)

The word 'decoy' comes from the Dutch and it was a gentleman by the name of De Koy who introduced us to the original duck decoy once so popular on our east coast and used by the old market gunners. Today, with the advent of cheap reliable plastics, the pigeon decoy is available in many different shapes and sizes. How different it was fifty years ago when virtually all that was around was the carved decoy made some- times with balsa wood, but more often from cheap pine. These were all bulky and often heavy. Shells made from aluminium were available but difficult to find after the war. Nowadays we are spoilt for choice, but always remember that most pigeon decoys are made with man as much as pigeons in mind.

I have probably used most of the commercial decoys on sale over the last twenty years and I would say that the best ones, in the long run, have been the lightest. If there is one great truism in decoying it is that whatever is easiest and doesn't break is going to be the most successful. Pigeon shooters in general are not minded to carrying too much weight for too long!

Half shells are always a good bet. They are easy to stack, light, and virtually unbreakable. The one problem that I have found with shells is that the sticks intended to support them and give them their movement are always breaking or getting themselves lost. Full-bodied decoys also come in a variety of sizes and weights, but I must admit that when I have to fill my game bag with a dozen of these, I always wonder why I bother. The main thing about plastic or rubber decoys is that they should be slightly bigger than life-size, painted the right colours, *in matt paint*, and equally important, they must have big enough white neck bands and wing bars to be clearly visible as flock recognition signals. It matters little if the decoy is a bit on the large size or that there is too much white showing, as long as it attracts the bird to within reasonable shooting range. Do remember that all the fine detail is added by the manufacturer to attract the decoyer into the shop.

When I first started decoying there were all sorts of old wives' tales about decoys, one of which was that you had to cut the eyelids off dead pigeons which you used as decoys so that the incoming birds could not tell that their friends on the ground were dead. The best story, however, is a relatively recent one. When I was writing the Pigeon Forum column for *Shooting Times* in the mid-1980s I used to have a sort of surgery one evening per week when readers would ring up with their pigeon problems and I would attempt to solve them. One evening a gentleman rang up to ask whether I knew the difference between male and female birds. I admitted that I could usually tell the difference, but only when the bird was dead, and then not always for sure without dissection. Never mind, he said, would I please explain the difference because he had a theory that if he put out ten birds he would do better if eight of them were female and only two were male!

Much has been said over the years about making your own decoys with a variety of materials, including dead birds cured with all sorts of unspeakable chemicals. However, I am of the firm belief that there is such a wide variety of commercial artificial decoys on the market today that I for one cannot be bothered to make my own out of grey plastic drainpipe or cure dead birds and stick their wings onto plastic replicas.

Without a shadow of doubt dead birds make the best decoys. Every self-respecting pigeon shooter should keep at least half a dozen dead birds in his freezer and take them out the night before he intends to go shooting. These dead birds should be used on lofted cradles of some sort and the rest of the pattern should be made up with plastics until enough birds have been shot to replace the latter. (If you are short of dead birds, mark the ones you use as decoys by cutting off one leg and then freeze and defrost them until they are completely unusable. Then leave them for the foxes.)

When setting up dead birds in the pattern they should be made to look as natural as possible. A useful aid for this are short sticks (around six inches long) taken from hedgerows. The sticks can either be straight or forked and should be pushed into the ground and used to support the birds' chins to simulate live feeding birds. Clods of earth, stubble stalks and stones are equally useful for this purpose. Do not have all your birds in the head up, alert position or your incoming pigeon will shy away from the pattern as his 'friends' will look as if they are about to take off. Every now and then it helps to open a dead bird's wings to show the white wing bars and give the passing pigeon more confidence in your pattern. I sometimes take a leaf out of Archie Coats' book and put one dead bird, with its wings open, ten yards or so away from the rest of the pattern and facing in the opposite direction to the other decoys.

I am aware that the pigeon shooter is quite often an avid gadget man and although I have nothing against this I think that some of us lose sight of what we are trying to do when out pigeon shooting, which is to practise fieldcraft and shoot pigeons. There seem to be more gadgets on the market than there are decoys. The main thing that any gadget must do is impart movement to the decoy pattern. It should ideally also give the decoy it holds enough height above the ground (or crop), to make it easier for the passing pigeon to see it from further away than a decoy placed on or just above the ground. Chris Cradock, that great doyen of the shooting world, has a dictum about decoys and movement: 'Movement in the decoys, not in the hide.'

There are string and electronically controlled flappers, wire cradles which loft the bird a foot or so above the crop, lofting poles and rocking cradles (including my own copyright version), all of which work to a greater or lesser degree, always provided that we use them as intended and not as some magic formula to get the pigeons to fly in range without the application of any brain power or fieldcraft.

Archie Coats had the right idea; he applied his formidable knowledge to the problem and came up with one of the best solutions which I have ever seen. Archie used what was to hand, namely dead pigeons, and created movement by breaking the wings of a dead bird in the hide and chucking it out of the hide to attract a passing bird which was not quite committed to his pattern. Not everyone who has tried this trick has been successful, perhaps I have been lucky, but it has nearly always worked for me.

The gadget with which most people seem to have problems is the flapper. The line from the hide to the contraption twenty-five yards away always seems to get caught up with the crop or the dog, and worst of all, many people flap too much and frighten the bird away. The trick is to twitch the wings only once or twice and then leave well alone. Too much fast movement of the wings represents fear, and to an incoming pigeon this is a sure sign not to come any closer.

My own rocking cradles are much easier to use. They took me three years to develop and the design parameters were simple: create a device which will hold a dead bird securely without any moving parts and which will, at the same time, impart natural flying type movement without being touched by the shooter. It also had to be possible to use it at least two feet above the crop. I use the cradles in virtually all decoying situations and I am quite convinced that they have increased my chances enormously. They are virtually unbreakable and consist of a simple flexible rod with a wire frame attached to hold the dead bird.

There are three reasons why these cradles work: first, the movement of the dead birds attracts the eye of passing pigeon, secondly they allow the incoming pigeon to use them as guides and a stop in the pattern by the position in which they are placed in that pattern and thirdly, because they show the decoys at quite a height above the ground, they are easier to see from afar off.

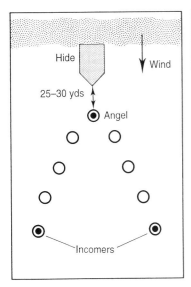 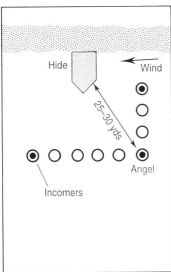 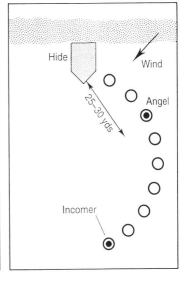

While I was doing the development work on my cradles, I used them in all sorts of different situations and in different places in the pattern. I finally discovered that three cradles seemed to be the optimum number to have in any one pattern, and consequently reduced the pattern to just three decoys. Three dead birds on cradles placed in the right position achieved virtually the same result as the dozen or more decoys which I had been using for years. It was slower, of course – three birds do not attract the eye as quickly as a dozen. But it worked, and it was from these early experiments that I developed my three criteria for all decoy patterns: Safety, Space and Salvation. When I am out on my own these days I still start the day with three dead birds on cradles, and they still work. I get an enormous buzz out of watching a single pigeon, a quarter of a mile away, turn and come back to my three-bird pattern. Sometimes they actually land in the pattern, just behind the leading decoy.

Virtually all cradle and flapper type gadgets have a number of things in common. They all rely on movement to attract the pigeon but, more subtly, most of them show the white wing bars, which as we know are a flock recognition signal. I firmly believe that the pigeon uses the movement of the wing bar to determine whether to join others or, whether to take fright and head for the hills as quickly as possible.

In 1988 I had the good fortune to make a video with Archie Coats, and during the editing sessions with Richard Duplock, the producer and director, we noticed that, in slow motion, there was a definite difference in the attitude of some pigeons to the pattern than others. For example, if I missed a pigeon which was settling into the decoys, thus causing very rapid wing beats to help it escape, any other bird which was approaching the decoys would turn away rapidly and avoid the pattern. If, however, the pigeon was shot and fell naturally to the ground, the second bird would usually keep coming into the pattern.

The advantage of slow motion film is that you can rewind whenever you want and, if necessary, check every wing beat. It soon became evident that woodpigeon use their wing bars as a means of communication as well as for flock recognition. Rapid movements appear to mean fear or danger, whereas slower movements mean that all is well. I was therefore able to set the open wings of the birds on my rocking cradles to a position which would entice the pigeon to my pattern. The results, as far as I am concerned, speak for themselves. It is already well documented that pigeons use their white neck bands to show their fellow birds if they are in danger when feeding. If you watch a feeding flock, just before they all fly away, you will notice that most of the heads are up and the neck bands are prominent. If, however, there is no

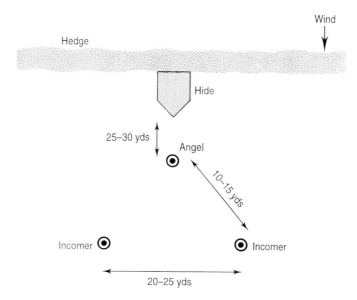

Three bird pattern

danger, the neck bands are much less prominent and the heads are all down as the birds are feeding

This section of the chapter would not be complete without a mention of lofters. First let us look at the extendable lofting poles which are usually employed to lift decoys twenty feet or more into branches of trees. These lightweight aluminium poles are, in my opinion, really only of any use when you are trying to attract pigeons to a particular tree when roost shooting. They can be very effective for this purpose especially if you are on your own and cannot cover more than one area of the wood at a time. Fire a shot in the wood and all the pigeons which have parked themselves out of your sight and range will go up. Then, with a bit of luck, they will circle over the wood and drop back into the branches alongside your lofters.

To use lofters when decoying near or on the edge of a wood is, to my mind, a waste of time. I have noticed over the years that any pigeon which appears to be approaching my decoys but settles in a tree rather than coming down to them is one that I shall never get. They either fly straight into the pattern or into the tree. Rarely have I seen a pigeon which has stopped short of the decoys and flown into a tree, then come from the tree down to the decoys. If they don't have the confidence to start with they usually fly away fairly promptly. Lofters are intended to attract pigeons to trees, and that is just what they do. What I want is a decoy which attracts an incoming bird to my decoys and not into a tree.

A serious word of warning. Every year we seem to lose at least one pigeon shooter who has been electrocuted by holding his aluminium lofting poles too close to high voltage power lines. Apparently your poles do not have to touch the actual wires for you to be electrocuted, as the current, at that voltage, can easily jump twelve feet or more. Be careful!

When lofting decoys in a pattern on a normal field, people will often ask me how high they can put their decoys without frightening the pigeons. The answer, very simply, is as high as the pigeons will tolerate without becoming frightened. A pigeon, in my opinion, does not have the reasoning power to work out that the pigeon which it sees floating two feet above the pattern is a dead bird attached to some sort of cradle device. What it will notice is a fellow pigeon apparently flying down to feed with a number of its own kind. Occasionally, because of an incline in the field, an incoming bird will approach the floater from below and jink away instead of coming into the decoys. What I think happens is

that as the incomer approaches on monocular vision and changes to binocular vision in order to land, it sees in front and above the silhouette of a bird which it mistakes for a predator, so it jinks away as fast as possible. If this is happening to your pattern take out the cradle and lay it flat on the ground and see what difference this makes.

Another use for lofters is over laid corn. You are nicely set up near a patch of well laid barley with all your decoys in the laid patch and the pigeons coming in quite well, when suddenly for apparently no reason, the birds divert to another laid patch 300 yards away and completely out of your reach. What you need is some sort of lofter to attract them back to your patch. I use a couple of old ex-army Jeep aerials into which I push my normal cradles. I use these contraptions up to about eight feet above the ground, with two or three of them to create a flight path right to my laid patch and the decoys in it. If the height of the decoys frightens the incoming birds I lower the cradles until they start coming in confidently. Decoying is essentially understanding what the live birds want to do and, with the aid of decoys, helping them do it.

A simple three or four foot bamboo cane costs only pennies and will work very well as a lofter. Break the wings of the dead bird fairly close to the body and spike it right through the body up into the head. Hold the bamboo cane, with the bird attached, up in front of you, as if you were carrying a flag pole in a procession, and move around until the wind opens both broken wings. Stick the cane into the ground at about forty-five degrees and watch the birds come straight into it. From the hide the whole thing looks a mess, but the pigeon see the flash of white wing bar in the breeze and turn into the pattern very well.

The only truly difficult decoying situation, where none of the rules seems to apply, is on fields of oilseed rape in winter when the birds are flocked up. We have seen how flock birds move as a flock, and not as individual birds. They will even establish special 'winter rape flight lines' which are different from their normal flight lines. It is no good seeing a large flock of birds on a field and thinking that you are going to have a bumper day. What usually happens is that you get a few shots and then the birds move *en masse* to another part of the field or, worse still, to another field altogether. This unfortunately is winter pigeon shooting over rape.

What can you do about it? Usually very little, I am afraid. You can try to follow the birds by moving your hide with the flock. Hard work and not very effective. You always end up one step behind the birds. What we have to do is understand that the pigeons *will* behave differently when they are in a flock, and if you go to where they are on the ground you will normally get very little return for your efforts.

The only sensible solution to the problem that I have come up with over the years is to watch the birds as they arrive, determine their flight line and go as far away down the flight line as you can, several fields away if possible. The reason, as ever, is straightforward. When the birds are on the line flying towards their chosen field to eat, they are not in a flock but in small numbers, normally four or five together. Build a hide under this line (it matters little what crop you are decoying on), put out some decoys and tempt the birds down to your decoys in ones and twos.

Imagine that you are going to see a very popular film at your local cinema. The auditorium holds over 2,000 people and you have to get there early and queue right around the block to get in. You are in your seat watching the film when suddenly there is a very loud bang in the cinema. What happens? Panic, of course, tremendous panic as everyone tries to flee. And, of course, after the panic has died down, no one returns to the cinema that day. Now, imagine that the explosion occurs while you are in the queue still several hundred yards away from the cinema, and that it happens not far away from you. What do you do this time? If you and your immediate companions in the queue are not injured, you will probably re-form the queue and move forwards again until you finally reach the cinema. Apply these principles to pigeons and winter rape and you will see why I move back down the flight line to decoy my birds. It doesn't always work, but it is a lot better than moving the hide and chasing the pigeons all day. Whatever you do, don't give up. I have had some real bonanza days on winter rape, when the pigeons have just thrown themselves at the decoys for apparently no reason at all. On another encouraging note, the first year's results of the BASC survey show that more than one third of the pigeons shot by members are shot over oilseed rape during the course of the whole year.

Another thing pigeons do not like is getting their feet wet, especially in the heavy clay country in which I live. So when it is wet underfoot, keep off the freshly worked bare soil and the wet foliage of rape and look for grass fields and set-aside, anything, in fact, which is well drained and drier underfoot than the plough. They don't like getting their feathers wet either. In showery weather watch how the pigeons leave the trees immediately after the showers have stopped so that they can fly around and dry off.

Winter rarely brings snow in my part of England any more, but when it did I used to have great difficulty decoying on it. The reason, I think, was that snow, being white, reflects upwards and makes the pigeon 'snow blind'. They could, of course, see their live brothers and sisters because of their movement on the ground, but they were blind to my pattern of static decoys.

Crows and other corvids are often attracted to much the same things as pigeon and will often feed amongst or close to them, especially on freshly drilled fields in spring. So put a crow decoy somewhere in your pattern – not too close to your pigeon decoys, but on its own about fifty yards from the hide – and see what happens. Sometimes it works very well and seems to give the pigeons the confidence to come more readily to your decoys. At other times it appears to frighten the life out of the birds and nothing will come anywhere near you. Just watch the birds and you will soon learn what they want to see. So, given the basic rules of decoying, you should be able to develop your own techniques as your fieldcraft improves, and not rely too much on books and films. Just remember the guidelines: protection on the ground while feeding, room to get in, room to get out and movement in the decoys not in the hide.

As a final point it is well worth repeating that nature tends to take around twenty minutes to return to the status quo after any major disturbance, such as hide building and decoy layout. If I have done my reconnaissance properly and built my hide in the right place and nothing happens after half an hour, I usually pack up and move, convinced that I have got it wrong, and the pigeons have moved elsewhere.

Real bird decoy

SHOOTING

So, who am I to teach you to shoot? Well, I am not actually going to try and teach the art of shooting – there are many others more capable than me for that job. What I am going to do is try and give you some tips on shooting pigeons, especially from a hide.

We should already know the basics of shooting, but I will run through them none the less. To shoot well you need three things: a gun which fits you well and in which you have confidence; to be so familiar with that gun that you mount it in the same place in the shoulder every time; and a proven cartridge which, if you hit the bird, will always bring it down cleanly. It matters little to me what gauge the gun is, whether it has one barrel or two, has extractors or ejectors, is heavily choked or has no choke at all. The crucial thing is that you are happy with the gun and that it does the job it was intended for. We shall be looking more closely at guns later in this chapter.

The actual methods of shooting are threefold. Firstly, mount the gun behind the bird, find the line of the bird, swing through and in front of it and squeeze the trigger. Secondly, mount the gun on the bird, swing through and in front and squeeze the trigger. Thirdly, mount the gun in front of the bird, stay in front and squeeze the trigger. The first method is the classical one, and the slowest, the third the fastest, and the second is the one which I prefer. Whichever you choose, or are taught, stick with it and practise, practise, practise. I practise mounting the gun on a picture rail at home to keep up the muscle memory, and I know plenty of others who do the same. One of the other main criteria is that you should be able to concentrate 100 per cent on the target all the time that you are shooting. If you are under any sort of stress you will generally shoot badly. My own axiom for shooting well is that I should be relaxed enough to be able to concentrate completely.

Given that you already know how to shoot, what is so different about shooting decoyed pigeon? The main thing is that conditions are usually more cramped than on a formal game or clay shoot, and you have to rise to your feet and shoot in fairly short order. Your footwork will not be as good as you would like and your body will not be perfectly balanced. Furthermore, if you shoot sitting down, you will have no footwork at all. The birds may well present themselves at all sorts of angles, ranges and speeds, and all within a few minutes of one another. You may sit for twenty minutes with no action, then the gun will become too hot to hold for the next twenty minutes, and then the same process may well be repeated again. All of this cries out, to me at least, the message, 'Have a gun that fits!' Added to all this is the fact that pigeons are crafty little

AB.

Jinking

devils and it is very often almost impossible to read their speed. They will appear to float gently into the decoys at what looks like two miles an hour, and you will miss behind with both barrels because it was really ten miles an hour.

The question of lead, or forward allowance, in pigeon shooting has always been a fraught one. The close, 'over the decoys' shot appears to need little or no lead at all, but the best advice I can offer is the same as I was given many years ago by my uncle: 'Forget about the tail and body of the bird and concentrate solely on the beak. The bird only has a beak. Find it and get in front of it.'

The bird which comes straight at you when you have the wind behind you is an easy one both to hit and miss. Point straight at it and you will miss cleanly behind. Put the gun down for a moment and watch it. If it overflies the decoys towards you it will rise to get over either the hide or the fence behind you, so lift the gun with the bird, get in front of it, and you will hit it right on the beak. If it is committed to landing in the decoys, then simply mount on the bird and fire just before it lands.

With the crossing shot, a bird always needs more lead than you think; the further out it is the more lead you have to give it. For the going away shot, with a gun which fits you, simply mount the gun, float the bird over the bead and fire. A dead bird in the air every time! The high overhead shot. You shouldn't be doing this from a hide! Remember that the idea is to decoy the birds to your pattern and then shoot them at a sensible range. The sitting shot is one which you may never take. The choice is yours, but the shot is not an easy one. Shoot at the bird's feet with the choke barrel. Most shotguns shoot high, especially if shot as a rifle. If you shoot straight at it, the pattern will go clean over the top of it. With its wings folded close around it the bird has extra protection and needs a little choke.

When shooting pairs, take a leaf out of Archie Coats' book and let both birds come into the decoys. Let the first bird land, shoot the second as it comes in and then shoot the first as it gets up and flies away. Whatever the shot, remember that without some sort of forward allowance, the only way that you will hit the bird is if it stops in mid-air, and then flies backwards.

On the question of shooting prowess, here is a favourite anecdote from my own experiences. In May 1985, I took three young Frenchmen pigeon shooting over a field of peas. Two were paying guests and the third more or less tagged along for the ride. I set up the first two, who were quite reasonable shots, in separate hides, and things started to happen. There were lots of pigeons flying around and lots of bangs and pigeon were falling fairly regularly out of the sky. The third young man

AS.

Low into wind

also wanted to have a go. He said he was an experienced shot and produced from the back of his car an O/U Browning. We went off to the far end of the pea field and I built a hide for him as well. I set out the decoys and a bird or two started to come in. The Frenchman asked me to shoot a couple to give him an idea of the range and timing needed. This was done and he said that he would be fine on his own now, so I left him a bag of 100 cartridges and went off to see his friends.

From time to time during the afternoon I could see birds over his hide and hear the bangs so I looked after the paying guests and left him to his own devices. At around four o'clock I thought I had better go and pay him a visit to tidy up the pattern and collect any runners with the dog. On arriving at the hide I saw an enormous pile of empty cartridge cases, but no pigeon. When I asked where they were I was told that there were none. He had seen plenty of birds losing feathers, but there were none dead on the ground. He had five cartridges left, ninety-five fired and not a pigeon down! It transpired that the gentleman was a rifle shot and had never fired a shotgun in his life. He merely lifted the gun, pointed and fired. There is a moral of course. It was my fault for not checking more thoroughly his claim to be 'experienced'.

Although I said that I was not going to try and teach you to shoot, I cannot resist passing on two general hints. The two most common causes of missing are lifting your head off the stock and hesitating on the bird instead of shooting it. Shooting has a lot to do with confidence, and hesitating usually means lack of confidence. I remember being with Archie Coats in a hide when we made the video together and at some point during the day, very conscious of the Master's presence, I was missing too many birds. There was a rumbling from the back of the hide. 'You're dwelling on them, my boy. You've done it before. Stop it, and get on and shoot them!'

Shooting over decoys very often means shooting birds at head height, or even lower, on a regular basis. For someone starting out this is somewhat disconcerting. The safety angle is one of extreme importance and one which must be looked at carefully. Under normal circumstances it is unusual to shoot at a gamebird unless there is 'sky' around it, although walked up grouse, flighting teal and almost any shot at woodcock are exceptions. The big difference between these quarry and pigeon is that pigeon over decoys are usually shot at from a hide which is a fixed point. So the Gun is not on the move.

You should take great care to ensure that the field of fire from the hide is always worked out before the shooting starts. Are there any public footpaths or rights of way anywhere in range of the proposed hide site? Are you on a farm during the school holidays, when there are more likely to be children around? Is there any stock on the farm? Have you looked on the other side of the hedges, before you put the decoys out? In short, as you are shooting low, are you sure that your shot will not damage anything except the pigeons you are shooting at? Shot will travel several hundred yards and at 100 yards could have someone's eye out.

Safety also includes ear and eye protection. The message is short and very easy to understand: wear hearing protection of some sort, otherwise you will eventually go deaf. Eye protection, against stray ricocheting pellets, is also a good idea. Safety in the hide is important, whether it involves a lone shooter or two or more people out shooting together, and I have developed the following guidelines. Never, ever, allow more than one gun to be in use at any one time. If two people are present in the same hide then one person should be shooting and the other should have his gun in a slip and be spotting pigeon for the person who is shooting. It is common for two friends to share the same hide and quite easy for them to decide how long each one should shoot. It can either be until a particular number of birds has been shot or cartridges used, or a predetermined time. This aspect of hide

A3.

Dropping in

discipline is vital. Fatal accidents have happened, and will continue to happen, if these basic safety rules are ignored.

The need for constant vigilance is borne out by several incidents which actually happened to me. The first occurred when a friend and I were out shooting pigeons together in Gloucestershire. We had decided to take a gun along that belonged to my friend and with which he had only shot clays. He apparently had a bit of a phobia about shooting the gun at live quarry, despite putting up very high scores at skeet with it. Needless to say he missed nearly everything that he fired at and we exchanged guns to see whether it was his fault or the gun's. The weapon in question was an over and under and I sat with it in my hide, waiting for some pigeon to come into the decoys. After a while they duly obliged and I shot a handful. I was sitting with the gun across my knees and loading and closing it (stock to barrels) as usual, with the barrels pointing to my left and downwards, when suddenly, on closing the reloaded gun, it went off, missing the dog's nose by an inch or two, making a hole in the netting and scaring me witless in the process. Not being familiar with the gun I allowed myself to be convinced by my friend that I had held on to the trigger whilst closing the gun. I wasn't so sure. I went home a shaken man and put the incident out of my mind until, a couple of weeks later, the same friend phoned me. He had just come back from shooting a round of skeet and the gun had gone off on closing! He is a very safe shot and the gun was pointing at the ground. Nonetheless, we were both lucky to have the gun pointing in a safe direction when reloading.

The luckiest escape that I have ever witnessed happened on a pheasant shoot. At the end of a drive a colleague picked up a loaded cartridge which someone had dropped during the drive and slipped it into his own pocket with his other ammunition. On the next drive I was standing one peg up to his left when a bird came over. I called to him, he put the gun up and I distinctly heard the sharp click of a striker firing on an empty chamber. He brought the gun down, broke it, and was looking into the chamber when another pheasant appeared over the trees. I saw him quickly stuff another cartridge into the gun, mount and attempt to fire again. There was another click and the pheasant sailed on un-scathed. He broke the gun again and I walked over to see if I could help. He was as white as a ghost and held out his hand, speechless. In it were three cartridges, two twelve-bore, one sixteen-bore! We worked out what had happened. The cartridge that he picked off the ground after the previous drive, although the same colour as his twelve-bore load, was a sixteen-bore. His gun was a chambered three inch magnum and the smaller bore cartridge had disappeared down the chamber, where it had lodged. On pulling the trigger the firing pin had met no resistance and had broken. He had then loaded a twelve-bore shell over the top of the sixteen-bore one! By the time we had worked out what had happened we were both shaking and white-faced.

The next story concerns one of the commercial pigeon courses which I run for half a dozen people at a time. I take great precautions to find out how safe I think the participants will be once I get them into the field with guns on the second day of the course. That weekend I had only four people on the course and I reckoned that they were all pretty safe. The second day of the course is spent finding flight lines and then building hides and shooting. On this particular day, in mid-February, I took everybody roost shooting as a bonus.

When in a wood with little-known Guns I have a set procedure of posting people by certain trees with strict instructions not to move unless I say so. I then go walkabout and visit each Gun in turn. On approaching a Gun I blow a whistle, and the person concerned has to unload his gun and then hold up his arm so that I can clearly see that he has done so. I was getting close to one particular man and had blown my whistle when I saw a pigeon dropping into the trees near to him. I called out not to unload but to shoot the pigeon. This he duly did, and fired a single shot at the bird which fell, a runner, some 100 yards away from us in the wood. The Gun, at this point, very correctly unloaded the gun, a

side by side English boxlock, and held it up for my inspection to show that it was empty. I was still fifteen yards away in a fairly gloomy wood, but accepted the fact that the gun was empty (after all I had already decided that he was safe). I had a young dog with me and said that I would go and pick the bird to see how the dog was progressing. The Gun asked if he could come and watch the dog at work.

The gun, which we both knew was empty, was leant against a tree in order to avoid scratching it in the undergrowth, and off we went to pick the wounded bird. We came back a few minutes later with a happy young dog and a pigeon, and while we were standing by the tree with the gun against it, discussing the retrieve, the dog's tail, wagging furiously, caught the gun and I was just able to catch it before it fell to the ground. I was taught that every time I was either handed a gun or picked one up, the first thing that I should do was to break it to check that it was empty. So I opened the gun and found that there was a loaded cartridge in it, in the left-hand barrel to be precise. It transpired that the Gun, having been game shooting all season, had experienced a fault with the ejectors on his gun. Every time that he opened it a cartridge would eject from the left-hand barrel, whether it had been fired or not. Rather than miss some shooting during the season through having the gun fixed, the Gun had got into the habit of holding his left palm over the left-hand barrel every time he opened the gun. This way he avoided losing a loaded cartridge on the ground. By now, after a whole season, the habit was well ingrained and when the gun was opened after the pigeon had been shot, his left hand must have come up automatically to maintain the loaded cartridge in the chamber. It was my fault, of course; I should have been closer when the gun was opened and checked more thoroughly. We live and learn.

Let us now look a little more closely at the choice of a gun and cartridge for pigeon shooting. I have already said that the first criterion for a pigeon shooting gun should be that it fits its owner. We should now look at the person who is just starting out on his pigeon shooting career and wants to acquire a gun for the job. The ideal gun for shooting out of a hide is going to be one which will give its owner the best possible chance to shoot the number of pigeons he wants to with the least recoil and smallest number of runners possible. It must be easy to reload, swing fast on instinctive shots and be versatile enough to take both close and longer birds. It must have good balance and be short enough in the barrels not to get caught up in the net every time he takes a shot. As to its commercial value, I am very happy to shoot a 'London Best' from a hide, as I know that it will handle better at the end of a long and tiring day than a cheap mass-produced gun.

So, what gun would I advise a novice pigeon shooter to buy? First, I think a twelve-bore (you get more lead in the air with each shot), as expensive as you can afford. Then I would advise that it should be capable of firing at least two shots before reloading. Half the fun of pigeon shooting is to be able to take, and sometimes plan, left and rights. A single-barrelled shotgun is just not quick enough for those busy days. (The three-shot semi-auto is a special case which I will deal with later.) I would strongly advocate a gun with ejectors, rather than extractors. There is nothing worse than seeing the pigeon pouring in to your decoys when you are frantically scrabbling around trying to reload a non-ejector gun. I would also suggest that it should not be too long in the barrels – about twenty-eight inches would seem about right.

As far as chokes are concerned, you need to be able to take birds as close as twenty yards without damaging them, and you also need to be able to take a second shot at around thirty-five yards (or at a sitting bird if you so choose). This means first barrel improved cylinder, second barrel half choke. It should weigh between six and a half and seven and a half pounds depending on whether the gun is side by side or over and under. And that is the question! Which should it be, barrels in the horizontal or vertical plane? The answer of course is whichever you feel most comfortable with. Let us look at the pros and cons of both types. I have shot for many years with both over and under and side by side guns and they both have good and bad points.

The over and under, with its single sighting plane, is more pointable, the pistol grip and single trigger mean that (if you are right-handed) you do not have to move your right hand between shots. The fore-end is designed to be held firmly and you never need a hand guard, or glove, to protect you from hot barrels. On the other hand it is much slower to load, especially the bottom barrel. Its balance will never be as good as the side by side and, to my mind, it does not swing as well in a cramped situation. Even if the gun has a barrel selector, a single trigger is a disadvantage in pigeon shooting as well as an advantage. Very often a bird will come in and, just as you are about to shoot it, it will jink away so that you need the choke barrel at very short notice. In these cases there is nothing to beat double triggers.

The side by side is an easier gun to get on to a fast-moving bird, and in my opinion there is nothing as sweet to handle as a traditional game gun. It is faster to load than its vertically built cousin, and it is easier to sit in a hide with it broken across your knees. But it has its disadvantages, of course. The barrels get hot and difficult to hold, the double triggers require movement of the fingers and hand, and there is probably slightly more recoil than the heavier over and under.

Reconnaissance: perhaps the most vital element of pigeon shooting.

The author's optimum equipment for a pigeon shooting day . . .

. . . easily portable.

Hide building equipment including nets, poles, pruning saw, gardening gloves, pegs, bungees and carrying bags.

...l, conventional, four-pole pigeon hide . . . unoccupied.

The author's hide . . . occupied.

...ntional hide with shooter standing to take bird in front.

Note hands and face of standing shooter in conventional hide.

Even when standing, shooter is hardly visible in the author's 'V'-fronted hide.

In conventional hide, shooter is easily visible even when

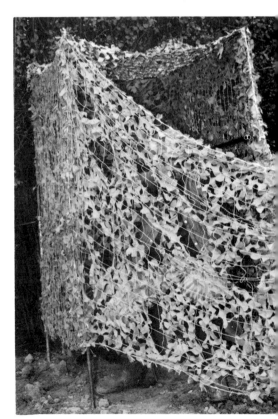

However, note the difference with seated shooter in 'V'-fronted hide.

Constructing 'V'-fronted net hide for guest.

Final briefing before the start of the day's sport.

Guest safely installed and waiting for the first pigeon.

How not to despatch a runner!   *Hold the bird like this.*

Twist the wrist inward . . .   *. . . and break the neck with a flick of the wrist.*

More effective and neater, hold the bird like this . . .

. . . and break the back by applying pressure

Raised side of hide makes it easier for the dog to get in and out.

Even the very best artificial decoys can sometimes shine in the sun and rain.

Make dead bird decoys look realistic by propping up some of the heads to show white neck bands. Note distinctive white wing bars.

White wing bars and neck bands show clearly on the author's cradles.

It matters little if your choice of gun be side by side, over and under or semi-automatic.

A good palombière *is far more than just a system of tunnels and huts in the woods.*

. . . it is also somewhere to enjoy the delights of the table and the vine.

The system of live decoys is complicated and requires great patience and experience to operate.

Some systems are so sophisticated that tethered birds can be induced to fly from tree to tree.

The author with one of the live decoys enjoying some entente cordiale *during a hard day's decoying.*

The choice is yours. Try out both types and buy the one that you feel happiest with. And remember that here we are looking at a gun specifically for pigeon shooting. Above all, use a gun that fits you well and one that you are happy with. For the last two years I have shot a side by side non-ejector twenty-eight bore, choked half and full. I shoot 9/16 of an ounce of No. 6 shot out of it, and have never had so much fun in my life!

I think that the semi-auto is a great gun for pigeon decoying. Several million Americans can't be wrong in their choice of shotgun! It has the familiar single sighting plane of the O/U, this time in single-barrel form, added to which it has a pointability which is legendary. I know of no one who can genuinely say that they have shot badly with it. It has virtually no perceived recoil and the third cartridge can be an enormous benefit on a busy day. The five-shot however, which these days requires a firearms ticket, has little place in a pigeon hide. The balance is awful and there are very few circumstances where five shots are either possible or needed.

For several years, in my early career as a professional pigeon shooter, I shot a Beretta 20-gauge three-shot semi-auto, and I can honestly say that it was amazing. It would pull down seemingly impossible birds time after time and, on one memorable occasion over freshly drilled spring barley, I managed to kill five flying pigeons with three shots! It was a fluke, of course, but the memory of it will linger long in my mind. I gave up the semi-auto when I started taking out guests. In those days I would build a second hide for myself and shoot after the guest had been installed in his own hide. I had several funny looks from people who had never been in the company of someone who shot a 'cowboy' gun, and as I was building the business, I gave the gun away and used an over and under instead.

It is sad, but many so-called sportsmen think that it is only the gun which is dangerous, not the person handling it. Of course guns are dangerous – after all, they are designed specifically to kill things – but I dislike being judged on what I shoot with rather than the way in which I conduct myself on the shooting field. A semi-auto has one big disadvantage as far as safety is concerned in that you cannot break it in the middle to see if it is loaded or if the barrel is clear of any obstruction. On the other hand, this can make the user of such a gun a safer person to be out with. The only way to check that there actually is no foreign matter in the barrel is to work the slide until the gun is empty and the slide remains open, then reverse the weapon and look down the business end of the barrel. I can assure you that you take more than extra care to ensure that the gun is empty before reversing it! The only other bad point about the semi-auto is that it throws out empty cartridges in all directions and often makes them difficult to collect at the end of the shoot.

My friend Guy Wallace tells a great story about the value of a good gun. A decade or so ago, soon after he got married, he had a problem. Money was in very short supply and his inherited shotgun had seen its last season and badly needed replacing. 'How much,' his wife enquired, 'is this new shotgun going to cost?' On being told that several hundred pounds was the price quoted, his wife merely replied that she could buy a washing machine for that amount of money. 'Would it not be a good idea to have a washing machine before a new gun?' Guy retired to the kennels to ponder on married life and finally came up with the solution. Over a judiciously large gin he again broached the subject of the new gun; after all the season was getting nearer. Marian again mentioned the dreaded washing machine and Guy dealt his trump card. 'A washing machine is all very well – but how the hell do you expect me to hit pheasants with a bloody washing machine?' He got his gun!

Enormous strides have been taken in cartridge design and manufacture since I started shooting in the 1950s, and things have changed beyond all recognition. Nowadays cartridges are faster and kill better than ever before. There is rarely a dud these days and the choice is enormous. As a general rule, for pigeon shooting, I would say that a one-ounce (twenty-eight gram) twelve-bore load will cover virtually every decoying situation. A twenty-bore cartridge need be no heavier than 13/16 ounce (twenty-three grams). Both these loads will kill pigeon more than adequately and will cause no recoil problems when fired from the average gun. As to shot size, I am not so sure as I was a few years ago. I used to use almost exclusively No.7 shot. Now I tend to use more No.6s, as I think that they stop the birds better and I get fewer runners. It may well be that now I have more experience I may be taking my birds a few yards further out than when I was younger. No.7s will give you more pellets in the air, and if you are doing all right with them, stick to them. If you find you are getting more runners than is acceptable, then change to No.6 shot. Cartridges are not really expensive, so do not stint on the price you pay for your squibs; buy the best that you can afford.

What is a good cartridge to kill ratio? The national average is probably one in four or one in five, so if you can manage anything under one in three *consistently* over the whole year, then you are doing well. But perhaps more important is whether you are happy with your own averages. If you are, then your average is a good one: if not, then it is a bad one.

AB.

Landing

Before leaving the subject I would like to suggest that we all think very hard about the type of wads we use in our cartridges these days. The majority seem to be of some sort of plastic and, although better results are claimed from ammunition loaded with them, they do leave a mess. Do we really need the performance that these wads give? Fibre wads may not offer quite the same performance but they are more than adequate for the ranges at which we are shooting over decoys, they are kinder to the environment and they certainly leave a lot less unsightly litter.

I used to take out two young Frenchmen who were two of the best shots that I have seen in my life. Jean-Luc and Patrick had been shooting pigeon with me for two or three years when they turned up one day with a challenge. I was to decoy the pigeon in to within twenty yards and they would shoot them with double-barrelled side by side .410s using a standard Eley fourlong cartridge. They shot 303 pigeons in three days with just over 600 shots! It just goes to show how the goal posts can move if you can shoot really well.

Should you sit or stand to shoot? Whichever you choose to do, the one thing about which I am adamant, in my own hide at least, is that I have a comfortable seat on which to sit and while away the idle hours. Shooting well depends on other things as well as the gun fitting properly, and one of them is keeping the body flexible. I know people who stand in a hide all day without ever sitting down and I am sure that they do not shoot as well at the end of the day as they did at the beginning. There is too much strain on the calf and thigh muscles if you stand all day.

It is far better to have a comfortable seat which allows you to stand and then sit down in complete comfort, without the seat tipping over. Equally important is to have a seat which is the right height and which does not put your calf muscles under constant stress as a shooting stick would, for example. Ideally, you should be sitting with your thighs parallel to the ground. Enter Batley's patent pigeon shooting seat. Like most of my equipment it is a development on what I have seen other shooters using over the years. In this instance, Archie Coats provided the basic design. He used an empty five-gallon steel oil drum, with a piece of binder twine through the handle for ease of carrying.

My own design is based on a modern twenty-five-litre sturdy plastic drum. I cut out a sufficiently large hole in the base to be able to carry decoys and the like inside it, and then put it, along with a sorbo rubber cushion, into an ex-army shoulder kit bag so that I can carry it easily across the fields. The beauty of the drum seat is that it has the same diameter at the top as the base so it will remain steady as you move around and not topple over as many commercially available seats seem to do. It weighs only a few pounds and doubles as a carrying bag. Although I say so myself, it is hard to fault! It is perfectly feasible to shoot sitting down from the type of seat which I use, as it is not prone to tipping over with the slightest movement. But shooting sitting down requires practice; there is no magic trick. Most of the problems are in the mind. You do not think that you will do very well sitting down, so you don't. If you try it you will find that you automatically learn to swing your body from the waist after a very short while, and the advantages can be considerable. The less you move in the hide, the less chance there is that the pigeon will see you, and therefore the more confidently they will come to the decoys. I do some of my shooting standing up and some sitting down, but I have to admit that I actually do shoot better standing up.

So far we have been discussing shooting from a hide. But what about roost shooting? When it is right there is nothing to beat it. You cannot load the gun fast enough, the birds keep pouring into the wood borne on a wild west wind and wherever you look there are more, and they are as fast and difficult as the most testing of driven grouse. Don't count the empty cartridges! When it is wrong you spend an hour and a half standing in a wet cold wood, all by yourself, only to watch the rooks and crows cackling their way home to bed while you haven't fired a shot!

I remember shooting pigeon off forty-foot towers in conifer woods in Aberdeenshire with John Darling, that brilliant photographer. Sometimes, when the wind was strong, they would skim the treetops in which we were standing and be almost impossible to hit. Other days, with not a breath of wind, they would be so high that we doubted whether we would ever bring one down.

The practicalities of roost shooting are quite straightforward. Pigeon like to roost in warm woods where they feel protected. They will usually choose mixed woods if they can – the ideal seems to be one where there are a number of trees mixed in with the conifers. The birds first come to the tall deciduous beeches, ashes and oaks to sit around and digest their last meal of the day, then, just before dark, they drop down to the branches of the conifers for the night. This way, they can see what is going on from their high perches whilst digesting and, if reassured, sleep confidently in the warmer, lower branches of the firs.

You need to watch your chosen wood over a few days to establish the line of flight into it on a given wind (west is usually best). You then need to know which of the high trees they will sit and digest in, which is very easy – just look for droppings under the trees. Now all you need to do is to establish yourself near a favourite tree and wait for the birds to come in to roost. Try and keep away from the outside edges of the wood, as you will be too easy to spot as the pigeons fly in. Choose a spot at least twenty yards in if you can.

There are a few dos and don'ts. Firstly, do stand with a tree at your back rather than in a clearing. Background cover will hide your silhouette. Secondly, be patient; wait for the birds to drop down to a shootable height. Thirdly, completely ignore any branches and shoot just as if you were in the open. There are enough pellets in your cartridges (only four or five are needed to stop the pigeon) for you not to have to worry about losing some of the charge in the branches. Fourthly, use a larger shot size than for decoying (six or even five). Some of the birds you will be shooting at will have their wings almost closed and the added penetration of the larger shot will do more damage. Fifthly, if you are going to shoot at sitting birds remember to shoot at their feet. Your shotgun shoots high when aimed like a rifle at a stationary target. The big temptation when roost shooting is to poke at the birds between the branches. Resist it! Swing, don't poke.

Next, marking your birds. The easiest way to do this in a wood is to choose a tree or bush in front of you before you start shooting and to use it as a reference point. Call your chosen tree twelve o'clock and mark your birds as they fall by the hours on the clock. If your memory isn't good enough, or you are very busy, use pieces of twig around your marker point. At the end of the roost simply use the imaginary clock to send the dog (or yourself) in the appropriate directions. If things are going well it will be almost dark when you finish shooting so you will need all the help you can get with picking up.

If you are roost shooting at the end of the shooting season, please remember the keeper (who has probably given you permission to be there in the first place) and do not stay too late. His pheasants still need to go up to roost even if they are not being shot at any more.

No section on shooting would be complete without the author reminiscing on some of the great days which he has had, and I am no different. Perhaps I have been luckier than most. I have certainly shot my fair share of game and a very considerable number of pigeons and I hope to go on shooting for a long time to come.

The first day that sticks out in my mind was in 1956 in Suffolk, the first weekend in February, and the first time that I participated in a winter roost shoot. It was cold, snowy weather and the pigeon, having been left alone all through the shooting season, came into the conifers with the dusk in complete confidence. I watched my uncle and two friends shoot over a hundred in about an hour. I can still smell the burnt powder and feel the warmth of the freshly shot pigeons on that first magical evening.

One of my other great days was in September 1991. On that day the deputy chairman of Holland & Holland, Roger Mitchell, was my guest in Herefordshire. We were to shoot pigeons with the prototype Holland & Holland over and under shotguns. There was a twenty-bore Royal sidelock O/U (No. 5001P) and a twelve-bore O/U trigger-plate lock. I am thrilled to say that I was the first person ever to shoot the 20 bore at live quarry and equally important, that first quarry was a woodpigeon, and it fell. For me, at least, a great moment of history and an enormous privilege. Since that day I have been fortunate enough to have been appointed by Holland & Holland as their agent in the west of England and I often have the opportunity of shooting their guns at my favourite quarry. It is sheer bliss! There is nothing like shooting a London Best at such a challenging target.

AB.

EQUIPMENT

Equipment for pigeon shooting is a subject which seems to cause as much controversy as the respective merits of particular famous sportsmen. I have seen people out on a day's decoying looking like an old-fashioned tinker, festooned from head to foot with more than enough gear for a small commando unit. On the other hand I have seen a genuine ex-commando with only a scrap of camouflage net plus his gun and cartridges come home laden down with pigeons.

Somewhere between these two extremes is the pigeon shooter who knows what he needs for a successful day out. The following is a list of what I carry when I go out, both with guests and on my own. But remember that it is not the equipment itself which gets the birds, but more the fieldcraft which is applied when using it.

1. Gun and cartridges. The gun is always in a slip, the cartridges always in a bag. I take a bag of 100 on to the field and I always have more locked away in the back of the vehicle, out of sight. I always carry a cartridge extractor in the cartridge bag and I carry a gun cleaning rod and equipment in the vehicle.
2. Hide and poles. My hides are permanently made up and the poles are attached to the nets. I usually carry a couple of extra poles on a windy day when I am out with guests. This stops the nets of the larger guest hides blowing about too much. The spare poles are the same light-weight telescopic aluminium ones that I use for all the hides. The hide is rolled up, held firmly in place with two or three 'bungees' and carried in a sturdy canvas shoulder bag of my own design, which will also carry thirty or more dead pigeons if need be.

3. Seats. I would rather be without the hide than the seat; comfort is all-important if you want to shoot well. Many times in the past I have crouched in a hide cursing the fact that I couldn't be bothered to bring the seat.
4. Game bag. This is the danger area! The bigger the game bag the more unnecessary rubbish you tend to take with you. This is what I think you need to carry in your game bag: decoys; lunch; first-aid kit; folding pruning saw; spare bungees; and an empty bag for used cartridges. In fact all these items, plus a sack for the dead pigeons, will go quite nicely inside one of my seats.

The folding pruning saw replaces the old-fashioned bill-hook. It weighs only a few ounces and mine has a Swedish steel blade which will cut anything I may encounter (at least in Herefordshire). 'Bungees', those wonderful inventions beloved of caravaners, replace the need for miles of binder twine and a knife to cut it with. 'Bungees' will act as guy ropes for the poles on a windy day, attach the poles to a hedge, fence or tree and generally make your life easier than it was before. Buy some now! The only other things I take out with me are three of my rocking cradles which, by the way, double as excellent nettle and bramble slashers.

The total weight of all the kit I carry works out at about thirty-two pounds, including the gun and 100 cartridges. Admittedly I mainly shoot a twenty-eight bore these days, but you need only add a couple of pounds for a twelve-bore. All the kit has shoulder straps and can be evenly distributed so that I can walk longish distances with relative ease. The idea of a trolley or similar device fills me with horror, not because of the devices themselves, but because of the people who use them. They will almost certainly be gadget mad, and not hunters, and this will probably be reflected in their decoying methods and their standard of shooting.

There are days, of course, when you are pretty certain that you will only get one or two birds and you really don't want to carry all that kit – a warm summer's evening perhaps, when a couple of hours of your own company away from the office will restore your sanity. In that case, this is what you need: your gun in a slip, two large pocketfuls of cartridges, three aluminium poles, a piece of lightweight camouflage netting, twelve feet by five feet, a seat, three dead birds, three cradles and a couple of the ever-useful 'bungees'. Strap the poles and cradles to your gunslip with your 'bungees', take a smallish piece of sorbo rubber, the net and the three decoys in a small game bag and off you go. On arrival at your chosen hide site, erect the hide in the form of a 'V' in front of you, with a hedge or tree behind you. Put out the three cradles, with dead birds attached, retire to the hide, kneel or sit on your piece of sorbo rubber and wait for the birds to trickle in. Great fun, and of course that will be the evening you could have got your first hundred ... if only you had brought the proper hide, seat and all the other paraphernalia.

What should you wear? Pigeon shooters are not known for their sartorial elegance – in fact, I would go so far as to say that pigeon shooting probably has a decidedly down-market image. This is not fair: the sport is as testing as any other where wild quarry is hunted. The knowledge and guile required to hunt the woodpigeon is certainly of a higher quality than that demanded of the average pheasant shooter standing on his peg. None the less, the image of 'Jack the lad' still persists, and it is up to us to do something about it. One of the easiest ways of changing that image is the way we dress.

Until about five years ago I used to favour the normal pigeon shooter's garb of ex-army camouflage clothing, but nowadays I dress as I would for any other type of shooting, that is breeks with a tweed or waterproof coat in the winter and a waistcoat in the summer. The result is interesting. When I first changed, the farmers on whose land I shoot nearly all asked why I was dressed that way. On being told that it was because of my respect for the quarry, I think they began to see the pigeon in a slightly different light themselves (at least I think it was the pigeon that they saw in a different light!). Perhaps more marked was the reaction of my clients, the majority of whom already had the respect for the quarry. They were happier to see their guide formally dressed.

If you build your hide properly, there is absolutely no need to wear camouflage gear. Remember that it is movement that alerts the pigeon to your presence, not your clothing. To test this, take a white plastic sack and put it flat on the field with the corners pegged down. After a very short while the pigeon will come and land all around it. Now attach it to a bamboo cane and let it wave around in the breeze. Until they get really used to it, the pigeon will shy away from the moving sack. I am not suggesting that we all wear white shirts for our pigeon shooting, simply that we try and think about our image as shooting people. Pigeon shooting is as much a 'field sport' as any other, but to gain the respect of the public (as well as our peers) we should dress and behave as well as any other participant in the more formal sports.

Although I do not believe that camouflage clothing is necessary in the hide, I do think that we should pay attention to those parts of our anatomy that the pigeon can easily see – our hands (and arms in summer) and faces. When you are out pigeon shooting with a friend, get him to stay in the hide while you walk two to three hundred yards away. Turn round and look back at the hide and its occupant. As long as your friend stays still your eye is not attracted to him. The moment that he moves his hands or face, you catch the glimpse of white straight away. A cap or hat will obscure the face from a distance, and gloves will not do any harm. But it is the movement that the birds see, so don't move until you are going to shoot. There is certainly no need for a face mask or veil.

My ideal clothing for shooting from a hide is something which is comfortable and weatherproof. Breeks and a tweed coat fit both these criteria, and I *always* wear a shooting waistcoat of some sort. I shoot better wearing a waistcoat, as it allows me to swing more easily. I also recommend full waterproof trousers in winter rather than leggings; it gets cold and damp in a hide in winter. As I have said, a hat or cap is a must to hide the face and particularly the forehead, but otherwise the choice is usually determined by the weather. I always carry a full change of clothes in the vehicle after the very unpleasant experience of falling down a snow bank one day and ending up in a stream, in which I was sitting up to my waist.

If you are a serious pigeon shooter, your car will probably be chosen with pigeons rather than wives and children in mind. If so, make sure that it is big enough for your hide poles and a large number of pigeons. I always carry about 1,000 spare cartridges with me (well concealed) along with my binoculars, first-aid kit, shotgun certificate, BASC membership card, maps, compass, water for the dog and towels for both the dog and myself. Another thing to keep in the car is a second gunslip, for when yours gets soaked. A gun which is wet and also has pigeon blood on it will rust extremely rapidly. The first-aid kit should have all the usual bandages, and something for wasp stings and mosquito bites, eye lotion and arnica cream for bruises.

Equipping yourself for pigeon shooting is rather like packing for a summer holiday – you always take too much! A good idea is to lay out your kit on the ground before you leave home and ask yourself when you last used each piece of equipment. Answer honestly, and pack accordingly.

CARE AND HANDLING OF BIRDS

Everyone who goes shooting, be it commercially or for the pot, needs to know how to look after the game which they have shot. This care starts with being able to dispatch runners. I have read many authors on the subject of killing wounded birds and, in the main, I think that they pander too much to the more squeamish among us by treating the matter as if it were a fairly rare occurrence. It is not. In pigeon shooting, for example, there are quite a

lot of runners – I would suggest about ten per cent of those shot. Wounded pigeons need to be dispatched quickly and efficiently, and I know of two ways to do this. The first is very fast, but leaves the bird with a broken neck. The second takes more time to learn, but when mastered leaves the bird in a more presentable state.

The first way is simplicity itself, but you will often end up being splattered in blood – if the bird is a runner, there will almost certainly be blood. Take the bird's head between the first two fingers of your hand, with your thumb on top of the head. Letting the bird hang downwards, twist your wrist inwards, towards your body, and then swiftly twist it outwards. This will break the neck inside the skin, the bird will die instantly, and the head will not come off. If you do not start with the inward twist of the wrist and merely twirl the bird by the neck you will nearly always separate the head from the body.

The second method is slightly more complicated but it has the advantage of not breaking the bird's neck, thus keeping the bird more presentable and you free of blood. Take the wounded bird, with its wings folded, firmly in your left hand, back uppermost, head away from you. Now run your right hand down its back until you reach the point where the wings fold. There you will find a small indentation. Push sharply down with your thumb into this indentation whilst forcing the head up and back with the left hand. The bird will die instantly, although it will twitch for a few seconds in nervous spasm.

You will notice that I have not mentioned using a priest for dispatching birds. While I have no objection to using one, I was brought up in the school which said, 'If you wound a bird, you yourself should be prepared to end its life.' After forty years of shooting I find no reason to alter this way of thinking. Whichever method you choose, however, you must be prepared to do it calmly and rapidly. If you are not prepared to do it, then in my opinion you should not be shooting. This may sound somewhat dogmatic, but I firmly believe it.

Let us now consider looking after the bag, both during the shooting day and afterwards at home. There are a few basic rules: empty full crops, keep the birds free from flyblow and allow them to cool before freezing.

Pressure Point

If you are roost shooting in winter, you will most likely be shooting birds with their crops stuffed full to bursting with oilseed rape. Before putting the bag away in the vehicle, therefore, empty all the crops. If you don't, and you go on to eat the birds, you will find that the meat has a sour taste. In fact I would recommend emptying the crops of all birds that you intend to sell or eat. Not only do you avoid souring the meat, you also find out what they have been eating, and that should tell you *where* they have been eating.

Flyblow is the only really unpleasant aspect of pigeon shooting that I can think of. In warm weather bluebottles like to lay their eggs somewhere where they will be most likely to hatch. One of the most favoured places is on meat, and what better place to find it than on a freshly shot pigeon! The newly laid eggs look, to all intents and purposes, like a small fresh pat of pale yellow butter. They are laid in any wound, particularly with blood on it, in the eyes, under the wings and, particularly, in the beak, and they have to be removed fairly smartly – in summer they will turn into maggots in less than thirty-six hours. The best way to approach this job is to de-fly them carefully at the end of the day's shooting. I don't advocate doing the job at home as wives can be funny about that sort of thing! If the beak or eyes are full of eggs then the best way to get rid of them is simply to remove the head.

I have tried everything I know, from fly sprays to keeping the birds in a portable game larder, to try and avoid flyblow, all to little avail. These days I just put up with the flies and make sure that the birds are individually checked before they go in the sacks to be taken home. They get checked again before they go into the freezer. On one memorable occasion I brought some freshly detached pigeon wings home with the idea of preserving them and sticking them on to some full-bodied decoys. I left them in a paper bag on a shelf over the back door and forgot all about them. My wife found them three or four days later, mainly by the smell but also by the way the paper bag moved, apparently of its own volition, when she went to pick it up. According to her, there were enough maggots to start a bait shop!

When you finally get your birds home, in pristine condition, there are one or two more things to do before either eating or selling them. Before freezing them, you should lay them out overnight, breast uppermost. This will allow them to cool and therefore freeze more quickly. If you are going to sell them, keep them neat and tidy for the game dealer. He will not take kindly to birds frozen in grotesque positions, and will probably offer you less for them as a result.

If you are going to eat your birds then you need to know a good way of preparing them for the cook in your household. (In our house, all game is given to the cook fully plucked and ready for her tender ministrations.) Pigeon makes a delicious meal and we eat several hundred every year, but to pluck and draw each bird is very tiring and since the best meat is on the breast, I normally take the breasts off the bird and either throw the rest away or keep it for making stock. There are lots of very quick ways to de-breast a pigeon. Mine is not the quickest (it takes two minutes), but I end up with presentable pieces of meat rather than some that have been torn off the carcass. Pluck the breast and then, cutting the skin at the base of the breast, peel off the skin from the base of the breast to the crop. Lay the bird on a chopping board, head away from you, and using a very sharp knife cut down either side of the breastbone. The next step is simply to fret away the two fillets of meat from the breastbone with your knife, starting at the rear of the bird and working towards the neck. Be careful not to nick any of the

A.S.

intestines when cutting the skin and you should end up with two neat parcels of a couple of ounces or so of meat and no mess. Four birds will make a good meal for two. There are many recipes for pigeon available, so I will not presume to add to this well-documented field. Suffice it to say that pigeon makes a terrific meal and it should be cooked either very quickly or very slowly.

An equally well-documented subject is the hanging of game before eating it. The preference in our household is for young pigeon, and they need to be hung for no more than a day or so in the early autumn months. Winter pigeon we hang for up to four days. But we have eaten birds on the day that they were shot and others that have hung for much longer periods without suffering any ill-effects at all.

DOGS

A dog is as essential to the shooting man as the gun he carries and, like the gun, he sometimes does well and sometimes badly with it. Some of us are natural shots and some of us are natural dog handlers. I am neither. I work very hard at my shooting and less hard with my dogs. I have been lucky in that Meg, my first dog when I began shooting professionally, recognised the fact that I was not very bright and did most of the work for me. Meg was an absolute star. A black labrador bitch, she came to me when she was four years old, picked an estimated 23,000 pigeons for me and, sadly but necessarily, was put down when she was twelve.

I now have a replacement for Meg. He is called Baldrick – don't ask why! Baldrick has an action reminiscent of a demented Hoover. I have seen him sweep a field at the end of a day's pigeon shooting and bring back a dozen birds which would otherwise have been lost for ever. His place is not really in the hide, where he fidgets and fusses if not enough birds are attracted to the decoys and shot. His place is really out with others picking duck in a wild foaming river or on a wet peaty grouse moor, where he can cover himself in muck and glory. He is a 'doer', not a 'waiter', but I cannot do without him.

Is the best dog for pigeon shooting a spaniel or a labrador? How do you choose? The answer, of course, is the same as when choosing a gun – it depends on what you are happiest with. There are advantages and disadvantages with all breeds, but essentially you should be looking for a dog which is prepared to wait patiently for hours and hours without much happening. There is not much need, if you are an amateur pigeon shooter, for your dog to have a fantastic nose or, come to that, a fantastic pedigree. Most of its retrieving will be done on marked birds and, in fact, mostly birds which are clearly visible.

What you do need, however, is obedience and some brain power. From an early age most dogs, if shown, will quickly work out which are the dead birds used as decoys and which are the freshly shot ones. A bit of patience on your part and a lot of enthusiasm should ensure that your dog will soon get the habit of only picking the birds you actually want back in the hide. On a slow hot day when my Meg would doze in the back of the hide, she had a wonderful system of working out which bird to bring back when she had not seen the bird actually fall. On being woken up, she would head, in her ladylike fashion, out of the hide towards the decoy pattern. She would approach the decoys from downwind and quarter the pattern until she found a fresh bird. If this was anywhere near the killing ground, which I like to keep empty, she would bring it back immediately. If it was elsewhere, she would put her paw on it and look hopefully back at the hide. All it then required was an encouraging word from me and she would bring it back. Sadly, there will probably never be another Meg for me.

If your dog is very young then I think you should start its pigeon-picking career very carefully. The one big problem with pigeons and dogs seems to be feathers. Pigeons have an enormous quantity of very loose feathers, which dogs obviously get in their mouths. They are difficult for the dog to get rid of, as dogs can't spit. After a while the dog will either learn to pick up the bird just below the neck or get fed up with the whole process and not retrieve pigeons any more. If this happens, remember that it is not the dog's fault. A useful hint is to wipe the dog's mouth clear of feathers each time you take a bird from it. I start my young dogs on dead pigeons wrapped in old tights. This seems to help a little but eventually you will have to give the dog the real thing and then it is up to it to cope.

Here are a few useful tips on working with dogs which I have picked up over the years:

1. Always have plenty of water available for your dog, in the hide in summer and in the car at other times.
2. Rape stubble is very bad for dogs' paws, which can get badly cut on freshly harvested fields. Soak the paws in a mixture of salt and water over a few days before taking the dog on to the stubble.

3. Swallowed feathers mean constipation. A spoonful of olive oil from time to time will fix this.
4. If your dog is hunting heavy cover, especially brambles and nettles in summer, smear Vaseline liberally around his eyes before he starts work and you will avoid cuts around the eyes.
5. If your dog really takes a dislike to pigeons and their feathers, which has happened to me, use him for something else or give him away. It is not his fault.
6. Buy your dog from a professional breeder or trainer who really knows what he is talking about. Tell him that you intend to use the dog for pigeon shooting and be guided by him.

On balance I think that perhaps the labrador is the wisest choice for the pigeon shooter. They seem to have a quieter temperament than the spaniel and are more willing to sit for long periods in a hide. The spaniels that I have known seem to be happier when on the move and not confined to one place for too long.

Everyone has their favourite dog story and I am no different, but my dogs have certainly been different. My wife has a Jack Russell (poor girl) with which I have a 'love-hate' relationship – I pretend to hate the dog, and the dog appears to love me! When my wife was in hospital with our firstborn I had charge of all the dogs, including the Jack Russell which had been out beating but never pigeon shooting, and I took them all for a day out over a field of peas. The labradors, of course, knew what to do, but not the J. R. She had to be firmly attached to my seat to stop her running in at every shot I fired.

Imagine the scene: two black labradors sitting placidly in the hide, taking it in turns to pick up the pigeons and a frenetic white terrier trying to get out to commit mayhem in the decoy pattern. All went relatively well until I stood to take a shot, winged a bird which fell in the pattern and started to walk off the field. Before I could put one of the labs on to the runner the Jack Russell, still attached to my seat, but with no other restraint, dashed out into the field dragging hide and seat behind her. The pigeon escaped and the dog got nearly fifty yards, festooned in nets, before I caught it. As I said, make your choice of gundog for pigeon shooting with extreme care!

I will end this chapter with an Arab saying told to me by Guy Wallace, an excellent trainer of gundogs. He picked it up in the Middle East and it was originally about hawks, but applies equally to gundogs: 'When your first dog dies, it leaves such a large hole in your heart that all the others fall through it.'

5

The Legal and Ethical Position

I n this chapter, I want to look at the laws and regulations that govern our sport, as well as such related subjects as all year round shooting, professional pigeon guides, the practice of feeding fields, the legal use of live decoys in France and the future of pigeon shooting.

The 1981 Wildlife and Countryside Act said that the woodpigeon was one of a number of birds which could be shot by authorised persons at all times (as long as you have permission to shoot on the land, you are an authorised person). Subject to certain restrictions as to how the bird might actually be taken (listed in Section 5 of the Act, and covering things like the illegality of using live decoys), this remained the case until the introduction of a General Licence on 1 January 1993. This removed the woodpigeon, and other birds such as corvids, from Schedule 2, Part II of the Act (but still subjected them to the same restrictions in Section 5), and brought them under an annual, general, renewable licence issued by the Department of the Environment. This licensing system was introduced to 'meet our legal obligations under the EC Birds Directive. It will provide the same basis for pest control as under the 1981 Act and will permit authorised persons to continue with their existing practices. Monitoring of pest birds will be an integral part of the new system and will help the Government to assess whether special steps ought to be taken to conserve any species where its decline was casting doubt on its ability to survive in the longer term.'

The General Licence under which we now operate is, in my opinion, another example of the interference of Brussels in our daily lives. I believe it came about through political rather than bureaucratic necessity. In 1990, various political factions in Europe decided that we should fall in line with the rest of Europe and have a closed season for woodpigeon – for nine months of the year!

The problem arose in September 1990 when the Government 'proposed to make certain amendments to the Wildlife and Countryside Act of 1981 in response to a letter from the European Commission stating that existing British law does not fully comply with the terms of the EC Directive of 1979.' In short, the Government, reacting to political and legal pressures from the EC, intended to 'transfer the woodpigeon from Part II of Schedule 2 of the Act, to Part 1 of the Act, thereby restricting its killing (other than under licence issued under Section 16 of the Act) to periods outside the close season. The close season for this species would be defined as 1 March to 30 November.' The proposed close season never came about. The BASC and other organisations mounted a supreme effort and the result is the General Licence which complies with the terms of the EC Directive and allows any authorised person to shoot woodpigeon all the year round – exactly the same as under the Wildlife and Countryside Act of 1981! It is a sensible document in my opinion, but one that is only as safe as the Government which introduced it.

A positive outcome from all this is that the BASC began a programme of research, in close co-operation with the Game Conservancy Trust, NFU and MAFF, to learn more about the importance of woodpigeons and woodpigeon shooting in this country. This programme involves shooting surveys, bag studies, analysis of ring recoveries and surveys of farmers' problems and attitudes. Both in the short and the long terms, this type of research will, I am sure, prove to be our main defence for field sports against the ever-increasing political pressures which now beset us.

I discussed briefly the ethics of year-round shooting in Chapter Three. But what about the ethics of paying a professional pigeon shooting guide to let you practise a wild bird sport without having done anything to earn that right?

I am, amongst other things, a professional pigeon shooting guide and my conscience is clear. I shoot all the year round for the reasons I gave in Chapter Three. I prefer not, however, to take other people shooting over laid corn and I actively discourage my guests from shooting the squabs which inevitably come to the decoys in the summer months. By taking people shooting who have no land of their own, or have no time to do reconnaissance, I provide a worthwhile service. Apart from making my living, I have the time to learn more about the woodpigeon, and pass on what I have learned to others.

I hear a lot of complaints about guides who cheat their clients. I think that the problem is not so much one of the guide cheating the client, as of the client deluding himself that the guide can turn on the pigeons, like turning on a tap, to order. I accept that there are crooks and charlatans, as in any walk of life, but I think that very often people expect too much of wild bird sport in terms of the bag at the close of the day.

However, there are a number of practices with which I am in total disagreement. Perhaps the most important of these, to my mind, is that of feeding or baiting fields so that an unscrupulous person will know where the pigeons are likely to be at almost any time. Pigeon decoying is about reconnaissance and hunting. Turning it into a predictable sport takes the hunting element away. Apart from the ethical question, there is also the possibility that feeding a recognised pest species might be construed as being against the law. In my view, too, it is cheating, and therefore defeats the object of hunting a wild quarry species. What is the point? You might just as well use live decoys – as they do, quite legally, in France.

HUNTING WOODPIGEON IN FRANCE

Decoying in France is a completely different concept from the one we know in Britain. I am not talking about the odd decoyer who has local government permission, usually around Paris or in the north, to shoot some pigeons as a crop protection exercise. This is about an art, a skill practised in the south-west of France, usually in les Landes, which involves the use of live decoy birds at the time of the great annual pigeon migration south to Spain, Italy and Africa. I have been there and I have to say that I not only agree with the concept and the methods, which include the use of live decoys, but also I think that it is one of the most difficult forms of hunting that I have ever taken part in.

Woodpigeon migrate southwards every year, crossing the Pyrenees in southern France and wintering further south. Millions of birds are involved in this migration, which starts in mid-September and ends halfway through November. They fly in flocks, which range from a dozen to a thousand or more birds. Before crossing the mountains they pass les Landes, the largest wooded area in Europe, and the French have a system of hunting them which is quite extraordinary.

In the open pine woods which abound in les Landes, they find themselves a small clearing which is under the birds' main flight line on their way south. There they build themselves a *palombière*. This consists of a large wooden hut, rather like a very sophisticated garden shed, with a hatch in the roof from which they can watch the arrival of the pigeons. They then make up to half-a-dozen tunnels which radiate outwards from the hut. These tunnels, some as long as 200 yards, are built from either metal or wooden hoops covered with bracken and acacia branches, and are usually about five feet high. The idea is to entice pigeon to the trees around the hut and the tunnels so that they can be shot or netted. To do this they use live decoy birds positioned in strategic branches, not unlike our lofters, to persuade the migrating birds to join the decoys in the trees.

They take a live feral or town pigeon, hood and jess it, attach it to a small seesaw-like device and haul it, through a system of cords and pulleys, thirty feet up a tree. Then, when they see a flock of pigeons approaching the clearing, they tug on the cord attached to the seesaw. The tethered bird will flap its wings to keep its balance, thus attracting the wild birds to come and join it in the tree. Some of the decoys are placed in trees up to 150 yards away from the *palombière* and the system of cords and pulleys has to work so smoothly that the slightest tug on the cord at the *palombière* will set the bird's wings flapping, sometimes without the operator even being able to see the decoy. Once the decoys are installed, the hunters retire to the hut. They open the hatch in the roof, sit on the bench just below it and wait. When a flight comes their way, they assess the direction of the birds and then tug on a cord, either to the right or the left, depending on the flight path of the approaching birds.

If they are lucky the migrating birds will welcome the rest and come and perch in the branches near the decoys. Leaving the cords attached to the bench so that the other decoys cannot flutter around, the hunter scuttles off down one of the tunnels armed with a shotgun. On arriving below the tree where he thinks the incoming bird or birds have perched, he pokes the gun through the tunnel walls and tries to shoot a bird – much easier said than done!

The harder way, and much more fun, is not to shoot the birds at all but to try and decoy them from the trees down to the ground and attempt to net them. This is where the real skill comes in. Migratory birds are incredibly twitchy – a few loose feathers on the ground, the snapping of a twig, the merest hint of movement in the tunnels, and all is lost. It can take two hours from the time the birds first land in the trees to get them on to the ground.

How they do it is by preparing an area roughly ten by twenty yards which is kept seeded and looks like a small lawn. Alongside this *sol* is a small cage trap with another live decoy inside. The hunter pulls a string from inside the tunnel and releases the decoy, which starts to wander about the *sol*. It is not tethered, but has been trained to feed on the maize which is put out for it. The hunter will by now have been calling and cooing to the birds in the trees for at least half an hour to increase their confidence. Now is the time for the *coup de grâce* – the final live decoy! This one is attached to a small 'T'-shaped perch about two feet long and hooded and jessed like the ones in the trees. Crouched in the tunnel the hunter takes this perch in one hand and, starting from about four feet above the ground, smartly brings it downwards, causing the bird to flap its wings to keep its balance. The sound of the fluttering of wings gives even more confidence to the birds perched above you and they come down to the *sol* to feed. When a few have alighted on the ground, the hunter releases the spring-loaded nets from either side of the *sol* and *voilà*, he has perhaps half a dozen birds in the net. In all the times at which I have been present in a *palombière*, however, I have seen no more than eight or nine birds caught at any one time, and more often than not a whole day passes without getting a single bird down to the ground.

One of my best friends in France is a man whose family has been practising this art for nearly half a century now, from the same *palombière*, and I go and visit Jean Loubere nearly every year. In 1993, over a nine-week period, he got seven birds, while last year, over the same period, he got 201! He has constructed nearly 1,000 yards of tunnels over the years. Jean has more than thirty live decoys which have to be hauled up the trees every morning at dawn and then brought down again at dusk, freed from their hoods and jesses, fed and watered, and replaced in their large coops. The whole procedure has to be repeated in reverse at dawn the following morning and it takes at least an hour to prepare for the day's sport.

The *palombière* teaches patience like no other field sport I have ever practised, and I cannot hope to do justice to the art of working the decoys with mere words. It also has other advantages. The reason for the substantial hut instead of a hide is very French, and one of which I heartily approve. Inside every *palombière* there are a table and chairs, a Calor gas cooking stove, at least one armchair, water, cooking utensils and, above all, a wine rack! The French family of a *chasseur* will meet at the *palombière* on Sundays and cook the most magnificent meals that you can imagine. I can recall one visit to such a *palombière* where I helped push a wheelbarrow through the woods at dawn in preparation for the feast to come at midday. In it were freshly picked mushrooms, home-cured ham, home-made bread, a haunch of well-hung venison, free-range chicken, fruit and vegetables galore, and I can't remember how many bottles of wine!

The French have another way of shooting woodpigeon at migration which I have also had the good fortune to practise. This involves mini-mountain climbing up to the cols through which the birds pass on their way to Spain. There, perched on precipices and cliffs, you stand in a shelter, rather like a grouse butt, but over five feet high, with spy-holes in the front, and, as the birds fly over you, you shoot them – going away. If you try and shoot them as they are coming towards you, they will see you before you can fire and lift out of shot as quick as a flash. Last year there was a wind so strong that I couldn't stand upright outside the blind. I fired three cartridges in the day. And they say that the French are not sporting! They are, but they are also stark staring mad – and I love them dearly.

Not only do I find the sport of other countries fascinating, but it also teaches one tolerance of other methods than our own. The future of our sport is inevitably tied up with that of our partners in Europe and we must learn about their way of going about things, in the same way that they must learn about ours.

There seems to be no doubt that our mainly sedentary population of woodpigeon is rising. Long may it continue to do so (although my farming friends might disagree). I hear mutterings from people from time to time that there aren't as many pigeons about as there used to be. I really don't believe this. What I think is happening is that, mainly owing to different feeding patterns, the birds move around as flocks in winter and are more difficult to come to terms with. Allied to this is the fact that there are some 300,000 people out there shooting at woodpigeon. The pigeon has become a much more difficult bird to decoy than it was when I started in the 1950s. In those dim and distant days we used strips of newspaper as decoys to make our patterns. Try it today and see what happens!

I do not want to finish this book either moralising or painting a picture of doom and gloom for our sport. I firmly believe that the pigeon population in this country will continue to offer us sport for many years to come. I think that woodpigeon will become warier and warier and therefore harder to decoy, but that does not distress me at all; I am a strong believer in fieldcraft and the need for it. Go out and practise it, enjoy the sport and its many rewards, and remember the most important rule: do your reconnaissance and look for pigeons in the air, not on the ground.

APPENDIX 1
Lead Poisoning and Pigeon Shooters

T he poisoning of wildlife from ingested spent lead pellets is not new. It has been known since before the turn of the century. It has become an issue, particularly in the USA, mainly over the poisoning of ducks, geese, swans and other waterbirds, but one of the earliest records is from Britain when, in 1876, a letter to *The Field* magazine reported some pheasants being poisoned after ingesting spent shot. Since 1900, however, many cases have been recorded of waterfowl being poisoned. Extensive studies were undertaken in the USA during the 1950s and 1960s, in both the field and the laboratory, to assess the extent of the problem.

It became clear that ducks, geese, swans and other birds were picking up spent lead pellets left in the muds after waterfowl hunting, in mistake for grit or items of food. Whilst many pellets were being voided in the droppings of these birds, the grinding action of the grit-filled gizzard, necessary for the digestion of their food, also led to lead being absorbed into the bloodstream. Lead is a toxic metal which has no known biological benefit. Once in the body, it affects many of the bird's systems, including the blood, muscle and nervous systems. Lead shot ingestion is fatal in some but not all cases, its toxicity varying with a wide range of factors. A duck ingesting ten or more pellets is likely to die within a few days with few signs of poisoning, but this is probably quite rare. More common is for a bird to eat fewer pellets and to die in two or three weeks after showing considerable weight loss, green stained droppings, growing weakness and inability to fly or even stand up. Frequently paralysis of the gizzard and gut muscle sets in, which prevents the birds from feeding properly and hence leads to starvation.

The studies in America led to an estimate in 1959 of some two to three million American waterfowl dying each autumn from lead poisoning. Concerns began to grow and calls were made to ban the use of lead shot in waterfowl hunting. A hunt for non-lead materials for use in shotgun cartridges got under way, but the only one to be developed and approved as non-toxic was steel (strictly speaking, soft iron) shot.

As early as 1972/73 the use of lead was banned in some American wildlife refuges and steel shot was used in its place. This generated some argument and controversy, with several lawsuits challenging the bans on lead shot over the following fifteen years. Then in 1986 the Federal Government adopted a policy of replacing lead shot throughout the country for all waterfowl hunting. It began a five-year process of phasing out the use of lead shot, which was completed in 1991. As no other material had been approved, despite some thirty-six different ideas being tried, steel shot was the only alternative available.

Whilst the focus of concern was very much on waterfowl, a wide range of other bird species in the USA was also found to be susceptible to ingested lead poisoning. The list includes waders, cranes, gulls, flamingos and divers, as well as upland gamebirds and birds of prey. The latter group was found to ingest the lead shot in the bodies of their prey which had either died from lead poisoning or been wounded during the course of hunting. Amongst the upland game-birds, pheasants and quail have been affected, and also the mourning dove. This species is a very important quarry species in the USA, and up to six per cent of birds were found to contain lead.

Not surprisingly, the findings in the USA led to studies being undertaken in other countries. In particular, studies in Britain in the 1950s, 1960s and 1970s all showed that lead pellets were being ingested by many different species of waterfowl. A study by WAGBI, the RSPB and the Wildfowl Trust from 1979 to 1981 revealed that eight species of ducks, two of geese and three of swans contained various levels of ingested lead in their gizzards, sometimes up to twenty per cent of samples but more usually up to about ten per cent. Analysis of livers, kidneys and bones, (tissues which reveal recent as well as prolonged exposure to lead), showed that many of these birds had tissue lead levels more than high enough to cause poisoning and death. More recently, in over twenty sites in Scotland and other sites elsewhere in Britain, swans, geese and some ducks have been found dead or dying from ingested lead poisoning.

Affected birds have been found on coastal sites as well as inland wetlands, including flight ponds and freshwater marshes. The number of lead pellets in the muds of shot sites vary considerably but have reached levels as high as or even (sometimes much) higher than those recorded in America and other European countries. Up to thirty pellets per square yard were found in the WAGBI/RSPB/WT study but, since then, other sites have been found with up to 400 pellets per square yard of mud, caused by both wildfowling and clay pigeon shooting.

For many years arguments have raged on both sides of the Atlantic over the numbers of birds being poisoned and how much it matters. Inevitably, in Britain, calls were made to ban lead as they were in America. During the 1970s and 1980s WAGBI resisted these pressures, arguing that the numbers of birds being poisoned were not sufficiently large to justify the change, particularly when there were no acceptable alternatives for use in place of lead in this country. In 1983, however, the Royal Commission on Environmental Pollution, amongst its many recommendations to reduce the impact of lead on the environment, recommended that, as soon as alternatives to lead shot were available, the Government should ban the use of lead for shooting and fishing. Only three years later the anglers found themselves facing bans on angling lead weights because of the losses of mute swans in many parts of southern England as a result of swallowing discarded fishing weights.

At the same time, pressures were growing in other countries to stop the use of lead shot in shooting. In Denmark, for example, losses of swans from ingested lead poisoning led to a phasing out of lead shot, beginning in 1984 over some coastal sites and flight ponds, and eventually covering virtually the whole country by 1993. In the same year the Dutch Government banned the use of lead in nearly all shooting in Holland, with little provision for phasing in the use of alternatives. In various other European countries the use of lead shot is also being increasingly restricted, particularly for waterfowl shooting, through either statutory measures or voluntary programmes agreed with the shooting organisations.

A particularly important meeting took place in Brussels in 1991. The International Waterfowl and Wetlands Research Bureau organised a major gathering of representatives from over twenty countries, at which the issue of lead poisoning of waterfowl was thoroughly addressed. As a result of all the evidence presented, the participants (which included many shooting, conservation, farming and governmental bodies) concluded that, in view of the widespread problems caused to waterfowl by lead, it should be phased out of wetlands as soon as possible. The British Department of the Environment decided that Britain also had to do something to reduce the use of lead in wetlands. In the autumn of that year it set up a working group to advise not if but when, where and how lead in British wetlands should be replaced and to prepare a replacement programme.

The arguments about the scale of losses of waterfowl from lead poisoning continue but the number of birds dying is less important than the fact that they are dying unnecessarily. This wastage of birds does not add up to the 'wise use' of our waterfowl populations and the BASC, the Game Conservancy Trust, The British Field Sports Society, gun and cartridge makers, farming and landowning organisations, all accept that these losses should be eliminated if possible. They are prepared to support the Government's replacement programme provided acceptable alternatives to lead are available and the replacement is not carried out too quickly or creates greater problems than already exist. They also recognise that lead contamination of the environment is a political issue and that removing lead from shooting is an easy measure for governments to take, to show they are addressing the environmentalist concerns.

The Government's replacement programme is aimed specifically at wetlands, to deal with the problem of waterfowl lead poisoning which has been demonstrated there. By September 1995 it was hoped to have a range of non-toxic alternatives to lead shot cartridges available in the shops for sportsmen to begin using over wetlands. All the main cartridge manufacturers have been prepared to provide alternatives and some cartridges, mainly of steel and bismuth shot, have begun appearing and have been tried by some people. It is not enough, however, to have cartridges available in the shops if they are not suitable for wetland shooting. The shooting organisations have always insisted that any non-toxic cartridges, to be acceptable, had to satisfy four key criteria.

First, they had to be safe. This means that the service pressures of the cartridges should not exceed the chamber pressures for which guns are proofed. 'Safety' also requires that the cartridges cause no damage to the guns through which they are fired. The second criterion is that such cartridges should be effective; that is, that they should have a lethality similar to that of lead up to about forty yards and not cause any increase in wounding of live quarry. The third is that the material from which the shot is made must be as non-toxic as possible, since there is little to be gained by replacing one toxic material with another which is likely to cause similar or other environmental problems in the future. And the fourth is that alternative cartridges must be reasonably priced, so that sportsmen will not be unduly discouraged from buying them.

Given that cartridges satisfy these criteria and become available for use starting with the 1995-96 shooting season, their use will be encouraged over any wetlands which are important for feeding waterfowl. This applies to coastal wetlands such as foreshores and saltmarshes, and to inland freshwater marshes, lakes, rivers and ponds, where the continued deposition of spent lead pellets could cause a risk of poisoning to the ducks, geese or swans using them. To begin with the programme refers only to twelve-bore shotguns, since these deposit the great majority of lead shot into wetlands and because the Government accepted that finding acceptable alternatives for larger- and smaller-bored guns would need more time.

An important achievement of the shooting organisations was to win the Government's agreement that the process of change should be a voluntary one, at least initially. It is likely, however, that if substantial progress has not been achieved within some two years or so of the start of this voluntary process, then the Government will be pressurised by environmental bodies to seek legislation to enforce the change. Unless there is a change of government during this period, it seems unlikely that any legislation would come forward until after 1997.

While the programme is specifically aimed at eliminating the risk of lead poisoning for waterfowl, it affects a wider range of people than the sportsmen and sportswomen who shoot ducks or geese over wetlands. There are many game shoots and clay shoots, and no doubt some pigeon shoots, where the spent lead shot does fall into wetlands which are regularly used by waterfowl. It is hoped that these sportsmen will also help towards solving the problem of lead poisoning by either using non-toxic alternatives or, perhaps, by making adjustments in the way they conduct their sport so that their lead no longer falls into those wetlands. Such measures might include changing some game drives, reorientating clay pigeon traps or repositioning guns and decoys during pigeon shooting. The waterfowl/lead poisoning issue tends to be seen as a coastal one, but in fact the evidence shows that there is more lead and more exposure to lead poisoning from inland sites than from the coast. Sportsmen as a whole need to address this issue and contribute to its solution. The Government will be undertaking a monitoring programme from 1995 onwards to see how quickly lead replacement occurs. If it is seen that lead shot is still widely used on inland sites which are important to waterfowl, then the likelihood of legislation will increase.

Clearly, for this programme to be successful there needs to be a range of non-lead shot cartridges widely available, meeting the four criteria listed previously. Of the new materials already developed or shortly expected, steel shot (soft iron) is by far the most widely available. This is not to suggest that it is necessarily the best. It has a long history of development, having been used in the USA for twenty years, in Denmark for ten years and in other countries for shorter periods. Its cheapness, non-toxicity and ease of manufacture are in its favour. Its lower density compared with lead (around thirty per cent less) and its greater hardness (up to five times), however, have led to widespread concern about its ballistic effectiveness in the field, about whether it is more likely to wound rather than kill live quarry, and about whether its hardness will damage certain types of guns.

There is no doubt that steel shot does lose energy more quickly with range than lead shot. Consequently it may not be suitable for some types of shooting unless other adjustments are made. These include increasing the pellet size to increase the energy levels, and increasing the velocity of the shot cloud. The effective use of steel shot is influenced very much by range of the targets. Up to, say, thirty yards several steel shot loads already available in this country appear to perform acceptably well. Many gamebirds, wildfowl or pigeons, in fact, are shot at less than this range, so it may be that such steel shot cartridges will prove acceptable in place of lead for many shooting situations. Shooting larger ducks and geese at longer ranges, however, creates problems in building cartridges which are compatible with existing guns and yet still have the energy required to kill at these ranges without wounding. Much more development is needed in this area in this country.

Alongside these requirements is the need to ensure that the steel shot does not damage the guns firing it. The International Proofing Commission (CIP) has established new procedures and standards to ensure that steel shot cartridges do not cause damage to guns or risk of injury to the users. Provided the steel shot cartridges sold through gunsmiths have been approved by the British Proof Authorities as complying with CIP requirements, then there should be little risk to the user or the gun. The instructions on the cartridge boxes should be closely followed and advice sought if necessary from the gunsmith or the shooting organisations.

In all steel shot cartridges the pellets are contained in a hard plastic wad to prevent contact between the hard pellets and the barrel walls, which could otherwise result in the barrels being scratched. This will be seen by some as an unwelcome backward step, in light of the growing use of fibre and other types of degradable wads to prevent the littering of the environment with plastic. It is hoped, however, that biodegradable plastic wads will soon become available for use in such cartridges.

Much work is going on in Britain to test the effects of steel shot cartridges on the guns widely used in this country. Several studies have been conducted at the Royal Military College of Science (RMCS), Shrivenham, particularly for the BASC, to check the likelihood of the more traditional English game guns being damaged at the choke by the hard steel shot pellets encased in their plastic wads. This is one of the common concerns about steel shot. The risk of damage is greatest in lightly constructed guns at the choke cone where the bore of the barrel suddenly changes. None of the tests conducted so far by the RMCS has found this type of damage occurring with different types of steel shot cartridges. No guns which have been used with steel shot over the past few years in this country are known to have been damaged either. This is encouraging and suggests that the likelihood of this type of damage is lower than people have come to believe. It is very important to ensure that the steel cartridges are compatible with the gun in which they are used. As more tests are done and experience is gained, advice on matching steel cartridges with particular guns will become increasingly available from the cartridge manufacturers, gunsmiths, and shooting organisations.

The greater hardness of steel shot makes it ricochet more than lead shot. More care is needed in shooting, therefore, to ensure that people or property are not within range of ricocheting pellets. Care is also needed when eating game shot with steel since there is a greater risk of damaging teeth from the hard pellets!

There are several other materials which have been developed for use in shotgun cartridges, in place of lead and as an alternative to steel. A few years ago a tungsten polymer shot was developed by Eley Hawk, but it proved to be very expensive (up to £1 per cartridge, whereas steel shot cartridges are likely to cost up to about fifty per cent more than comparable lead shot cartridges), and had some ballistics problems. More recently the same company has developed bismuth, another heavy metal, into a wide range of shotgun cartridges suitable for guns ranging from two and a half- to three-inch chambers and loads from Impax No. 6 to Magnum 1½-ounce BBs. This development has attracted much attention and field tests are generally favourable. Concerns continue to be expressed about the limited supply of bismuth in the world and whether it is entirely non-toxic. This shot seems likely to find a use, particularly in guns where steel shot is possible or effective. Its cost, however, is likely to be two to three times that of lead.

Another shot type recently announced is made of molybdenum. This metal is mixed with other compounds to make a shot similar to lead in behaviour. It appears to offer the most lead-like performance yet, although commercial production of the cartridge has yet to get under way. It is likely to be much more widely available than bismuth, and without any concerns about toxicity. Its cost may also be lower than that of bismuth. A new shot based on tungsten has also been developed and cartridges containing it may well begin to appear towards the end of 1995. Other metals are also in the process of being developed in the shotgun cartridges but their details are still awaited.

It does seem, therefore, that a growing range of non-lead cartridges will become available from the 1995–6 season onwards. Their performance and characteristics will differ, as will their prices. They should offer a choice to shooting people with different types of guns and shooting interests, enabling them to find cartridges which are suited to their types of shooting, although almost inevitably, their cost will be higher than that of traditional lead shot cartridges.

It is one thing to welcome the appearance of non-lead cartridges on the gunsmith's shelf but another to know whether it is suited to a particular type of gun or type of shooting. This is where the research and testing which have been under way for several years, led particularly by the BASC, come in. Each shooting man and woman needs to know whether the cartridges which are available satisfy the criteria of safety, effectiveness, non-toxicity and price, particularly effectiveness. Accordingly, much effort has been expended in developing a means of testing the external ballistics of cartridges to evaluate their effectiveness in the field at killing live quarry or breaking clay pigeon targets.

A major new, and unique, ballistics measurement facility has been developed by University College, London and is sited on the Holland & Holland shooting grounds, Northwood. Funded primarily by the Government and shooting interests, this facility enables the external ballistics of any shotgun cartridge to be measured at any range from twenty to sixty yards in a way that has not been possible before. The energy of the pellets striking the target and the number of pellets likely to strike its vital tissues can now be accurately assessed. This enables each cartridge performance to be judged in terms of its lethality, compared with that of traditional lead shot. The Ballistics Research Laboratory is attracting growing interests from manufacturers of cartridges in this country and overseas as a means of helping them develop their own products, particularly of the non-toxic type. It also enables the shooting organisations and other interested parties to test cartridges to determine their characteristics and likely effectiveness for different types of shooting. Already this facility is providing a fascinating insight into the behaviour of shotgun cartridges and pellets in flight, and offers the potential to understand much more fully than before the importance of, for example, shot size, chamber length, choke degree and profile, and other components of cartridges, on their effectiveness at different ranges on different types of target.

What do these changes mean for woodpigeon shooting? In general, it should not be affected by the government lead replacement programme, the purpose of which is mainly to replace lead shot over wetlands. As little pigeon shooting takes place over wetlands which are important for feeding waterfowl, there should not be any great pressure on those involved in this sport, or in crop protection, to change to alternative materials. Furthermore, farmers have obligations to control pests on their land and this requirement has been taken into account in the development of the replacement programme.

On the other hand, it is important for the very large numbers of sportsmen and sportswomen in this country who do shoot woodpigeons, either for sport or to assist farmers, to be aware of the changes which are taking place and to see how they may be affected by them. Many people hold the view that, once a programme of lead replacement starts, although it may be restricted to wetlands to begin with, it will eventually spread to cover other or all types of shooting. This has certainly happened in other countries, and it could happen in this country, particularly following a change of government – although the Labour Party has indicated a willingness to be guided by the development of acceptable alternatives before requiring the replacement of lead shot.

The discussion about the effects of spent lead shot on the environment and wildlife will not go away. It will almost certainly increase. It is likely that, as people look for evidence of problems, they will find them. There have been cases already, in fact, of woodpigeons being poisoned by spent lead pellets in this country. These birds, therefore, are not immune from lead poisoning but the incidents appear to be rare. Another issue, however, is that of birds of prey being poisoned by eating prey which contains lead. Cases of this have been found in North America and France and some early indications show that it could happen in this county. If peregrine falcons, for example, were found to contain unusual levels of lead then the finger might well be pointed at their woodpigeon prey as being a possible source of that contamination.

The review of non-lead shot types given above gives an indication of some of the alternatives and options which the pigeon shooter will be able to consider, if he or she wishes, or is required, to change. On the basis of cost, steel shot is likely to be the most attractive alternative; the large numbers of cartridges often fired during woodpigeon shooting would require the cost of each to be as low as possible. Provided the guns being used are suitable – and many should be with the type of cartridge that would be appropriate – the other limitations of steel shot may not be too serious, particularly if the shooting is over decoys up to about thirty yards. For pigeon shooting under different circumstances or at a longer range, however, steel shot may not offer the pigeon shooter quite the performance that he is used to from lead. Time will tell whether improvements can be achieved by the manufacturers. With respect to the other materials likely to become available, such as bismuth, molybdenum or tungsten, their ballistic performance may well be closer to lead but the downside will be their higher cost. As with other types of shooting more directly affected by this programme of change, there is likely to be a choice of materials of differing performance and cost available to pigeon shooters.

There are other aspects of this whole issue which the pigeon shooter needs to bear in mind. In this world of environmentalism and green politics, there are growing concerns about contamination of the environment and the foods that we eat. Standards of quality and safety are being tightened all the time, often under European Union laws. This means that the input of shot from cartridges into the agricultural environment may come under increasing scrutiny. The deposition of lead in agricultural soils is one area which is attracting some attention, as is the fact that some crops are effective at trapping spent pellets before they reach the soil, leading to the possibility of foodstuffs being contaminated and livestock affected if they consume the pellets during their normal feeding. While concerns are likely to be higher if the material used is lead, they may also extend to other shot materials used in the future in place of lead. This, in turn, may lead to more restrictions on pigeon shooting, brought about by the concern of the farmer with regulations beyond his control. The growing interest in organic farming, for example, highlights the attention being given to maintaining the purity of the soil and growing environment for crops destined for human consumption.

There is another aspect which may well affect not just pigeon shooters but other shooting people also. There is a timber growing industry already established in this country for furniture veneer and a newly established industry growing poplar and similar trees on wet farmland for building and packaging materials. Echoing the experience of Danish timber growers, following the advent of steel shot in their country, timber growers in Britain are concerned about the consequences of embedded steel pellets in timber on both its market value and the cutting machinery in the sawmills. Already there are signs of landowners contracted to supply such timber from their land imposing restrictions on the use of steel shot anywhere on their land in order to prevent their wood being rejected by the sawmills. The industry will probably need to be reassured that non-steel shot types also do not pose any risks to their business or equipment before allowing traditional shooting on their land to continue once lead shot is no longer acceptable.

Overall, therefore, the prospect of change from lead shot is not welcomed by the shooting community in Britain. The problems it will bring are not of the shooting man's making but have been brought about by a mixture of political and biological pressures. There will be increasing pressure on the shooting fraternity to find alternatives to lead, even at higher costs and some disadvantage, if sporting shooting is to continue much as before. The pigeon shooter is certainly not at the forefront of this process of change but may be caught up in it as time goes by, or in specific areas where a change from lead has been required. It is not the end of the sport, however, although many people make it seem like that. Non-lead shotgun cartridges have been used in other countries for many years and the sport continues. Their development here will gather more momentum and a greater choice of type and performance will become increasingly available. Guns will become increasingly more suited to steel shot and other shot types will be quite compatible with existing guns. There is certainly a substantial change coming to the sport of shooting as a whole, but there have been other changes in the past and the sport has survived. In this instance there is no reason to doubt that, as long as there are large numbers of pigeons damaging farmers' crops – as there is every prospect of there being for many years to come – the opportunities for the enjoyment of pigeon shooting will continue despite the pressures against the use of lead shot.

Dr John Harradine
Head of Research, BASC

APPENDIX 2
Guns and Shooting

W hat is the ideal gun for pigeon shooting? How should you choose it and how should you use it? First, any bore size, from twelve right down to twenty-eight-bore, should be quite satisfactory. Then the gun must be fuelled correctly and the birds shot at within range – preferably thirty-five yards. You should always arrange both a trial shoot and a fitting of the gun before you buy it. It should be a first-class fit and comfortable to shoot.

These precautions are well worthwhile. Only your own body is capable of telling you whether a gun is comfortable to shoot. Equally importantly, by shooting at a few clays and at a pattern plate, you will know whether the gun, when mounted and pointed correctly, shoots anywhere near where you are looking and pointing it. A gun that is well fitted to its owner will feel just like an extension of his front arm and hand, and will point exactly at the target at which he is looking. However, the shooter must play his part and mount the gun in exactly the same position in his shoulder pocket from which the fitter took his measurements to produce the fitted gun. This will help him to point the gun muzzles exactly where he is looking. In other words, a well-fitted gun will allow the shooter's front hand, together with his gun muzzles, to follow his eye and so point accurately at the target. He will do this quite without thinking – in fact this movement should be as natural as breathing. With a well-fitted and well-mounted gun the hand should always follow the eye and so point the gun accurately.

For well over a century most British game guns have been stocked and fitted to throw their pellet patterns slightly high. This allows most shooters to obtain a better perspective of the muzzles and so a more accurate point. To check the fit of one's gun, many textbooks advocate standing sixteen yards in front of a pattern plate, then smartly bringing the loaded gun up from the ready position into the shoulder pocket and firing as the butt homes into place in the shoulder. However, many people find smooth gun mounting very difficult. Most gun owners make it hard for themselves by never practising their gun mounting. As a result, they do not mount their guns accurately and smoothly into the correct place in their shoulder pocket. Such a sloppy gun mount results in a misplaced pattern nowhere near the target. Such poor gun mounters would therefore be better to stand sixteen yards from the pattern plate and pre-mount the gun, taking a rifle-like aim at a mark on the plate. Fire a total of six shots, all at the same aiming mark. The result, when shooting a well-fitted, well-mounted gun, should be six pellet patterns all on top of each other. When this happens, you can be sure that the fit of your gun is good.

Re-whitewash the plate and stand with the loaded gun out of the shoulder in the usual gun-down position. Looking at the target, bring the gun smartly up into your shoulder and fire. Do this six times, and if the patterns are all on top of each other as happened with rifle-like aiming, your gun fits and your mount is accurate. If you are not placing pattern on pattern as you did when you rifle-aimed the gun, there is only one thing wrong – sloppy gun mounting. You have just proved that your gun puts pattern on pattern when pre-mounted, but not when you bring it up in one motion and then fire. The remedy is practice and more practice. Take a gun which you have checked is empty and stand in front of a mirror. Practise your mounting until you can achieve accurate butt placement in the shoulder pocket every time. When this is achieved, and with the eye looking straight down and slightly over the top rib, you should be able to mount and shoot a loaded gun so accurately at the pattern plate that the results are as good as when the gun was rifle-aimed.

Having got the gun fit and mounting technique perfected, you should practise at a shooting school on a decoy pigeon layout, but using dropping clays coming into the decoy pattern to perfect your technique for shooting settling birds. To break the clay, all one does is to move the gun slowly down, with the clay pigeon seeming to sit on the muzzles. When shooting real pigeons, you should be constantly aware, through your peripheral vision, of the settling pigeon's little pink toes seeming almost to sit on the muzzles as you slowly move them down. At that instant, pull the trigger. After the first bird has been shot, there may often be a second bird flaring up and away from the decoys. One can therefore swing up and through the bird; the slight inbuilt lead of a slightly high-shooting gun gives a better perspective, which is an advantage.

Whether you buy a double gun, side by side, over and under or a semi-automatic with a short magazine to make a total of one cartridge in the chamber and no more than two in the magazine, matters little. Correctly fitted and used, all these types of gun are suitable. Whichever you buy, however, it will be a great advantage if it is fitted with interchangeable, screw-in tubes. If you already own a gun with integral chokes, there need be no problem; there are firms which can custom-bore, thread and supply interchangeable chokes. For most average shots, a boring of improved cylinder in one barrel and no more than half-choke in the other is ample for decoying pigeons. In fact, for a lot of decoying, cylinder and improved cylinder should be found adequate for birds taken at up to thirty-five yards. However, there may be times when you have found a good flight line and set up a hide underneath it. On some flight lines the birds will be quite high and you may well prefer a half-choke tube. With practice you will soon acquire the experience to make a choice of the most suitable tube to suit the ranges at which you are taking pigeons. Judging flying heights does require experience; many shooters handicap themselves by believing that the birds they are attempting to shoot are within range when in fact they may be fifty to sixty yards high, which is really out of range.

Years ago, W. W. Greener said, 'There is no substitute for placing the pellet pattern on the bird. This is essential.' I have proved many times that to obtain clean kills one *must* place the pellet pattern on the *front* end of the bird. If one does this and the bird is within forty yards, an average of five size seven pellets from a normally loaded shot cartridge will have the energy to kill any pigeon cleanly. Those who try and shoot their pigeons at the rear end should go to a good shooting school and learn how to shoot efficiently and safely. They will be taught always to look at the bird's head, and then, by holding well forward, they should be able to trace the trailing edge of the pellet pattern consistently on the leading head of the flying pigeon. It is essential that all who shoot pigeons do so humanely and efficiently out of respect for the quarry. The original pigeon shooter's creed was, 'Shoot a bird and pick it up.' To shoot at all pigeons regardless of range is reprehensible.

It must be understood that after it leaves the barrel, the shot travels in a sausage-shaped cloud of perhaps thirty inches in diameter, and at a distance of thirty yards it will have a length of shot string amounting to about ten feet. Therefore it behoves us to err on the long side with our forward allowances. If we provide too little forward allowance, the whole of the shot charge passes behind the bird's tail and inevitably results in a miss, whereas if the lead is slightly too much, the pigeon may well fly into some part of the shot string.

Pigeons are reputed by some people to carry a lot of shot, with the result that they are difficult to kill. This erroneous idea is held even by some who should know better. It is true that when pigeons are plucked they surprise many sportsmen because they look so small without their feathers. One sporting writer of the last century wrote that the actual body was only about the same size as a claret glass. It is also true that the pigeon's feathers are fairly loose and easily fall out, so that even one pellet through a few feathers on the outside edges of a pigeon's body may give one the illusion that the pigeon has been hard hit when in fact only a few feathers have been dislodged. Most pigeon shooters feel better with this excuse rather than accepting the unpalatable truth that their own marksmanship is often just not accurate enough – and I am no exception! Anyone who doubts this should spend a few hours watching John Batley's technique. When he is in full swing, the pigeons he fires at usually come down dead enough, whether he is using a twelve- or a twenty-bore gun. That is because he is putting five pellets on the head of the pigeon.

You can load the dice to help you when shooting if the hide is a good one. You can then expect to lure pigeons into your decoy pattern while you sit well concealed. You ought to be sat well back in the hide and yet be able to mount, swing and fire while still sitting down. If you are well enough concealed, you should usually be able to fire at least one shot easily at a slowly settling bird before the noise of the explosion alerts others. By this time, if you know your job, the bird you have shot at will be dead anyway. This technique is obviously much better than the one so often used of lumbering to one's feet as the birds are coming in and appearing like a jack-in-the-box over the front hole in the hide. If you do this, the pigeons see the movement and immediately jink, flare and wheel away, turning into a curling, swirling, rising projectile, which is more difficult to shoot.

It has been proved many times that ordinary good-quality lead shot, as loaded in standard modern cartridges of size 6, 6½ or 7, has enough pellet energy to break a pigeon's wing at distances of up to forty yards. It has also been established many times that five pellets of these sizes placed on the front end of a pigeon will prove lethal up to the same distances. As my friend Bob Brister used to say, 'It is not the hard hitting which matters, it is the actual *hitting*.'

Finally, remember that certain precautions are never regretted. Good shooting etiquette is based on good manners and common sense. Never shoot where you cannot see. Shooting from a well-constructed hide as outlined in this book should allow you to kill the incoming bird before it is even aware of your presence.

To summarise, keep your eye on the bird, using your peripheral vision to see exactly the muzzle-to-target relationship. This lets you call your shots more accurately. Shoot sitting down if you can, take birds well within range and only shoot birds so that they drop where they can be easily picked up. Good, safe shooting.

Chris Cradock

Index

Index